AND HOW TO BRING OLD BOOKS BACK TO LIFE

Acknowledgements

Thank you to all of my friends and family who have helped me with this book, your help and support has meant so much to me.

Thank you to my husband who has never stopped believing in me and my abilities, your love and support sustained me through this process.

BOOKBINDING

AND HOW TO BRING OLD BOOKS BACK TO LIFE

AIMEE SPILLMAN

WHITE OWL

AN IMPRINT OF PEN & SWORD BOOKS LTD.
YORKSHIRE - PHILADELPHIA

First published in Great Britain in 2021 by
Pen & Sword WHITE OWL
An imprint of
Pen & Sword Books Ltd
Yorkshire – Philadelphia

Copyright © Aimee Spillman 2021

ISBN 9781526773784

The right of Aimee Spillman to be identified as Author of this work has been asserted by her in accordance with the Copyright, Designs and Patents Act 1988.

A CIP catalogue record for this book is
available from the British Library.

All rights reserved. No part of this book may be reproduced or transmitted in any form or by any means, electronic or mechanical including photocopying, recording or by any information storage and retrieval system, without permission from the Publisher in writing.

Printed and bound in India by Replika Press Pvt. Ltd.
Design: Paul Wilkinson

Pen & Sword Books Limited incorporates the imprints of Atlas, Archaeology, Aviation, Discovery, Family History, Fiction, History, Maritime, Military, Military Classics, Politics, Select, Transport, True Crime, Air World, Frontline Publishing, Leo Cooper, Remember When, Seaforth Publishing, The Praetorian Press, Wharncliffe Local History, Wharncliffe Transport, Wharncliffe True Crime and White Owl.

For a complete list of Pen & Sword titles please contact:
PEN & SWORD BOOKS LIMITED
47 Church Street, Barnsley, South Yorkshire, S70 2AS, England
E-mail: enquiries@pen-and-sword.co.uk
Website: www.pen-and-sword.co.uk

Or
PEN AND SWORD BOOKS
1950 Lawrence Rd, Havertown, PA 19083, USA
E-mail: Uspen-and-sword@casematepublishers.com
Website: www.penandswordbooks.com

Contents

INTRODUCTION:	What to expect from this book and how to use it	6
THE BOOK:	Its origins and etymology	7
GLOSSARY:	Terms used in bookbinding	11
	List of suppliers	15
CHAPTER ONE	Pamphlet Binding	16
CHAPTER TWO	Intermediate Bookbinding	48
CHAPTER THREE	Upcycling Your Existing Books	88
CHAPTER FOUR	Paper Repairs and Cleaning	104
CHAPTER FIVE	Weekend Projects	116

Introduction:
What to Expect From This Book and How to Use It

WELCOME TO BOOKBINDING FOR BEGINNERS, I'm Aimee and I will be your guide through the wonderful world of bookbinding, repairs and upcycling your books. This book will guide you through the basics, help you have fun and let your creativity flow.

In each chapter I have listed the tools and materials you will need and explained what we will be doing together over the next few pages. Within the instructions I will ask you to occasionally read ahead a few steps to help you get to grips with what we are going to be doing. Where I ask you to, please do this as it will help you out, especially if it's your first time. I have also left space in some sections for you to make notes. This is for you to note down what went well and what potentially didn't. It is then useful to read through these notes before you start again so you can get to grips with your strengths and weaknesses. .

This is a beginners' guide; the repairs I talk you through are beginners' repairs. If you have books that require extensive work please take them to a professional bookbinder like myself to carry out the restoration work. The repairs I have given you will keep your book going for a while and the paper repairs are the same process I would do; just with different tissue.

There is a range of ideas and crafting techniques for you to get to know. They are potentially different to what you are used to so please take your time and be patient with yourself. Improvement will come from practice and learning from mistakes – and you'll never know unless you give it a go, so why not? Above all, have fun! This is a craft not a lot of people are able to do and it can have a bit of a dry reputation, I hope this brings you as much joy as bookbinding brings me every day.

So be inspired, be creative and see what you can create.

The Book:
Its origins and etymology

A BRIEF HISTORY OF THE BOOK

Originally, scrolls were used to keep records on. In Egypt, scrolls were made from papyrus (see origin of the word paper), which provided large flat sheets to write on that could then be easily rolled up. These large flat papyrus sheets lent themselves to being attached to one another to create larger sheets that were then folded rather than rolled; this was a more efficient use of space and also made them easier to use as you didn't need to unroll the whole scroll to get to the information required, you could just look at each page.

Dead Sea Scroll at Qumran, Israel.

Johannes Gutenberg and a page from the Gutenberg Bible.

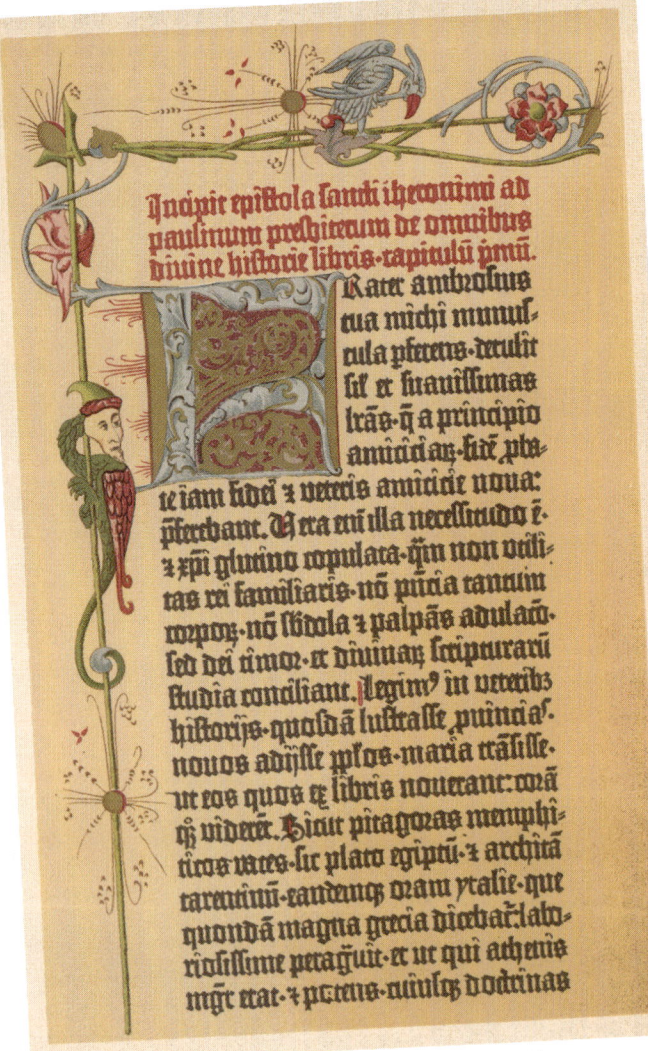

Paper was invented in China around 100BC, however, it took until the 1100s for paper to be manufactured in Europe, with the first paper mill being opened in Xativa in Spain in 1144. Before paper was manufactured in Europe, vellum was used. Vellum is calfskin which has been stretched and treated to make it very strong, but it is also quite stiff. Vellum is very susceptible to changes in atmospheric humidity and therefore is a nightmare for conservators. Paper also suffers when kept at different humidities, but it is a lot easier to control. Paper was lighter, cheaper and easier to mass produce than vellum, so it quickly replaced it as the material of choice for record keeping.

The printing press came along in the early 1400s, created by Johannes Gutenberg who used it to print the Gutenberg Bible. This was printed in folios (single sheets folded once); it was the first mass-produced and affordable Bible. Before the printing press, each copy of the Bible was hand-scribed, which took a long time. Gutenberg changed the way information was recorded and more importantly how easy it was to share. The printing press changed the way societies grew and aided in the mass literacy of populations; instead of hearing your scripture being read out, it was now accessible to you in your home.

In my opinion, paper and the printing press are amongst the most important inventions to shape society. They have aided in the growth and development of science, medicine, technology, business and the sharing of skills and knowledge – as demonstrated in this book.

The oldest-known bound books are leather-covered papyrus books called the Nag Hannadi codices. They are from the fourteenth century and are the world's oldest complete and covered books. Resembling what you might imagine a travel journal to look like, the leather is wrapped around the books and then they are attached to the cover with leather strips rather than being sewn on, as is common now.

St Cuthbert's Gospel (which you can see at the British Library) is the earliest surviving example of European binding. It has hard covers and the book is block-sewn with the boards attached. It was discovered in 1140 and has been dated to some time in 720–730AD.

ETYMOLOGY

I love etymology, the study of the history of individual words, their origins and how they came to be used. It is a fascinating subject, and bookbinding and books have their own fair share of interesting meanings and origins. I did my research for this section by reading *THE BOOK* by Keith Houston and using the online resource: www.etymonline.com

Book (noun)
The origin of the word book came from the Proto-Germanic of bokiz, which means beech. This refers to the wooden tablets filled with wax that predate paper in Europe. The tablets were attached to each other along the long edge and looked much like modern-day books do now.

The French use livre from Latin *librum*, the inner bark of trees.

Codex: manuscript text in book form.
Roman writers referred to wooden writing tablets as Caudies and later Codices – meaning tree trunk or block of wood. Codex was initially only meant to describe wooden writing tablets but over time it became the all-encompassing word for tablets made from any material.

Folio: Mid-fifteenth century from the late Latin folio: leaf or sheet of paper.

Latin – *Foolum*: Leaf.

Folio is also used when formatting books: a folio refers to a book or pamphlet that is made from a single sheet of paper that has been folded in half.

Recto Folio – Latin
On the right side of the leaf (so the side that's facing you in a book)

Verso Folio – Latin
On the backside of the leaf.

Library (noun)
Latin **Librarium**: book case, chest for books
Libraria: a book sellers shop
Liber: the inner bark of trees

Page (noun)
From around 1580, a Middle French word derived from the old French Pagne meaning page, text.
  Pagina: page, leaf of paper strip of papyrus fastened to others.
  Pagination: the act of marking up pages in order of binding
  Pagella: small page
  Pangene: to fasten
  Pag: to fasten

Paper (noun)
Directly from Latin Papyrus: paper made from papyrus stalks. From old French Papier: paper document.

Parchment (noun)
From around 1300, parchemin: the skin of sheep or goats prepared for use as writing material. Also from Pergamum (modern Bergama), the city in Mysia in Asia Minor where parchment supposedly first was adopted as a substitute for papyrus in the second century BC.

Tomes
A word used now to describe different parts of one larger set of books, came from **Tomos**, meaning small book or section from the Greek 'to cut' (from cutting down large scrolls into shorter ones to make them easier to store).
   Romans later called these Volumen from the Latin *evolver*: to roll out ready for storage. Scrolls were placed in stone or wooden jars for storage: this was Bibliotheke in ancient Greek; Bibliotheca in Latin.
   Hence we have the following, all meaning library:
   Bibliotheque – French
   Bibliothek – German
   Biblioteca – Italian
   Bibliteca – Spanish
These scrolls had labels attached to them to detail the contents inside. Greeks called these labels *Sittybos*; a misreading later translated this to *Sillybis* and thus into Syllabus. Romans called their labels on the scrolls *Titulus* and thus becoming Title.

Vellum (noun)
Old French Velin:– parchment made from calfskin (Vel/Veel = Calf)

Glossary:
Terms used in Bookbinding

BOOKBINDING, AS WITH ALL CRAFTS, has its own terminology. Some are obvious in their meaning, others are most definitely not. Here is an explanation of words and terms often used in the process of bookbinding.

Awl: Item used by bookbinders to make holes in paper. They come in a variety of thicknesses, try and get one that's a similar thickness to your needle.

Bookbinding material: This is the material backed with tissue to stop it stretching and allowing too much glue to permeate through.

Bookbinding thread: Linen thread used specifically by bookbinders as it is thicker than usual embroidery thread and made from linen, not cotton or silk. It's longer lasting and harder wearing so your book will last longer.

Book block: The main part of your book, so in this case the plain paper you have chosen.

Bone folder: A tool used by bookbinders for most procedures. As the name suggests, bone folders used to be made from bone, but they are now mainly made from Teflon or plastic. Teflon is a better material as it does not leave marks on the paper or leave any trace elements behind, which is especially perfect for conservation work. I find my bone folder is just an extension of my fingers, so it gets worn down rather than my fingertips. Each bookbinder's bone folder is specific to them; if you placed ten on a table and asked me to pick my own out, I would be able to as it is very specifically mine – not only has it bent to my hand but has also worn down in a specific way because of how I use it and what I use it for. No two are the same and it's always interesting to compare other bookbinders' bone folders to see the amazing difference.

Case: This is what goes around your book block and can come in any shape and size and be made from any material. Usually hard covers, but you can also use a thick card to make a case. Most books are case bound: the case is made separately from the book.

Endpapers: The decorated pages at the front and back of the book. These are what attach the book block to your boards so need to be strong. The side that gets stuck to the case is called the 'paste down' as it is pasted down (or PVA-glued down in our case).

Fore-edge: The edge that can be opened, otherwise it's the spine.

Grain direction: This refers to the direction the fibres are lying in a sheet of paper or grey board. This is very important when working with paper as all paper has a grain. Take one piece of paper and bend it both ways, one after the other. One of these will bend more easily (you are not folding, just bending). The way it bends most easily is the way the grain goes, so the long fibres that run through paper are all lying that way and this is the way you want to fold the paper. You'll need to cut your paper appropriately as it's important you go with the grain and not against it. This will be easier in the long run when folding, sewing and glueing.

Long Grain – fibres of your paper are lying along the longest length of your paper, so if an A3 sheet of paper is long grain once it is cut in half to A4 it's now short grain.

Short grain – the fibres are lying along the shortest width of your paper, so if A3 paper was short grain once cut in half it would make long-grain A4 paper.

Grey board: This is what your covers are made from. Grey board is made from coarse fibres that have been pressed together to make board and it comes in varying thicknesses, from 0.5mm up to and beyond 5mm. It can be purchased from large art supply shops like Cass Art and Paperchase. Within the book I will refer to grey boards and boards (boards once grey boards have been cut up).

GSM: An acronym for grams per square metre. This allows you to know how 'heavy' the paper is: the higher the GSM, the heavier and better quality the paper is.

Head and tail: This is how bookbinders refer to the top (head) and bottom (tail) of books.

Head and tail bands: These used to be an integral part of the book's structure, helping to attach the book to the case by being sewn through the boards and on to the book block. Now they are more for decoration, made off of the book or hand sewn on to the book block itself.

Japanese tissue: This is lightweight but very strong tissue paper. It has very long fibres allowing it to be a low gsm. I typically use around 9gsm as it is perfect for doing paper repairs. To do paper repairs, use it with paste rather than PVA as paste is reversible, water soluble and dries more slowly, giving you more time to work with the tissue.

Kettle stitches: These are always the first and last stitches when sewing up a section book. They are what hold the tension of the book and help to keep the sections attached to each other.

Knocking up: This is the action of banging your finished book block on a table to line all the sections up at the spine and push any rogue ones into line – it's like shuffling papers as a news reporter – just slightly harder and with more intention.

Leaves: These are the folded single sheets of paper bound in a book – each leaf forms two pages.

Link stitch: A form of sewing with sections – what we will be using in this book as we won't be sewing on to tapes or cords. The link stitch attaches each section to the last by having the thread link up with the previous stitch at specific points along the sewing.

Page: One side of a leaf of paper – so all leaves have two pages – if a book has thirty pages that means it has fifteen leaves of paper.

Pamphlet sewn: This is the method we will be using initially. It is a pamphlet because it is a whole book made from one folded section rather than multiple sections.

Paste: This comes in a variety of forms, wheat starch being the most common. It is fully reversible so I use it a lot when doing restoration work.

Pencil casing: This is a term used for when you haven't rubbed your material down enough and have left small air bubbles along the edge of your boards.

Perfect bound book: The most common way of binding modern books. Single sheets of paper are glued together at the spine and then covered in a card cover.

PVA: Poly Vinyl Acetate is a common glue used in a lot of crafts; it goes on white but dries clear. The benefits of PVA is that as a rubber-based glue it's flexible, making it perfect for glueing up spines as it bends with your book opening rather than cracking like paste does.

Sections: Section sewn books are made up of folded leaves of paper. Each section is normally twelve pages, so six leaves: three sheets of folded paper.

Section sewn books: Books were always section sewn before the invention of Perfect Bound books. The technique is still around today but generally used for high-end publications and one-offs. The books are made from paper being folded into multiple sections, then sewn up. This is a stronger way of binding books as each page has been sewn through and it also allows the book to open flat whilst not having to worry about pages coming loose.

Smoke sponge: Made of vulcanised rubber and perfect for cleaning surface dirt off your pages. It is frequently used in restoration and conservation work as it cleans the page without leaving any residue on the page. I have also seen it in pet shops to remove hairs from furniture!

Square: The space between the edge of your book block and the boards; the square is usually the same around all three sides, it cannot be at the spine as there is no gap here.

Weaver's knot: This is a knot used to combine two lengths of thread together. It's not practical or possible to sew a whole book with one length of thread – it would just be too long.

Suppliers

General bookbinding tools and materials, papers, materials and board.

Shepherds:
www.bookbinding.co.uk

LCBA
https://londonbookarts.org/

Patterned papers specifically great for endpapers.

Jemma Lewis
The most wonderful marble paper
www.jemmamarbling.com

Alphablots
The most glorious brightly coloured papers out there!
https://alphablots.com

Rifle Paper Co.
Whimsical papers in beautiful pastels.
www.huebow.com/collections/paper-decorative

Noi paper
Lovely papers with lots of women on them.
www.noipublishing.com

Suppliers of material and paper for your book blocks.

Winters
www.winter-company.com/en/products-a-z

Artway
www.artway.co.uk

CHAPTER ONE
Pamphlet Binding

THE MAIN THING I hope you will learn in this chapter is how fun and rewarding bookbinding is, and hopefully this will spur you on to the other chapters in this book. I really recommend you complete this section first so you get to grips with the basics and learn the language used in bookbinding.

You will be making a pamphlet sewn book; this means we will be sewing up a single section with the endpapers sewn on as well. Usually books (if they are sewn) are sewn in multiple sections to make a thicker book; when books aren't sewn, like in common paperbacks, this is called perfect binding.

The paper you use for your book block is important: too thin and it will tear easily when you sew your book, too thick and you will not be able to puncture it, so choose a paper around 100gsm. Your endpapers can be whatever you want, just be wary of handmade papers as they have a tendency to allow glue through the gaps in the fibres, so for your first few attempts I recommend sticking to machine-made papers. Do not use wrapping paper from rolls or paper that is shiny (it is a nightmare – it is too thin and will curl when you come to stick your book in).

Grain direction is important when you are sewing and glueing paper. If you have a piece of paper that is landscape and if the grain direction is left to right, it is long grain. However if the grain direction is head to tail, it is short grain. What grain direction means for paper is simply which way is easiest to bend/tear the paper. The easiest way to see grain direction is in newsprint. So grab a newspaper and tear a page. It will most likely tear more easily going from left to right rather than head to tail. This is because newsprint is usually printed in the wrong grain direction as it is cheaper to print papers this way. However, you do not want to have your paper in the wrong grain direction as it will cause you a massive headache when you come to stick it in.

The best way to test the grain direction of your paper is to gently

bend it (as we do not want to go tearing up good paper!). Take a sheet of paper and have it landscape oriented, gently bend it one way (i.e. left to right) and then the other (head to tail). Which way gives the least resistance? Whichever way is easiest shows you the direction of the grain. You are after paper that is short grain: so when your paper is landscape the grain direction goes head to tail.

Your endpapers also need to end up being short grain. As you will probably be cutting them out from a larger sheet of paper, make sure the pattern goes with the correct grain direction. Do not be tempted to just use it anyway as correct grain direction, especially for your endpapers, is very important. The reason for this is because you will be adding moisture to the paper in the form of PVA. When paper gets wet it starts to expand a little, and with the grain direction going head to tail the paper can expand out from left to right. If the grain direction goes left to right it will expand head to tail and it will not be able to do this evenly as it will be sewn up. The sewing will stop the paper closest to the spine from expanding, causing it to expand at the fore-edge and crinkle, which you do not want to happen.

With your paper and your endpapers sorted, your grey boards for the case now also need to go in the correct grain direction. You can check the grain direction of your grey boards by gently bending them as well, or you may be lucky and get told their direction when you buy them.

For this project you will need to have the following tools and materials ready:

Bone folder
Thread
Needle
Scalpel
Cutting mat
Scissors
Awl
Ruler
Pencil
Paper for your book block – this needs to be A5 so you make an A6 book.
Endpapers
Grey boards 2mm
Bookbinding material
PVA

Glue brush
Waste paper
Rectangle of paper for drawing on (10cm x 2cm)
Paper to use to line the spine (just some brown paper)

We will begin with making your book block so you'll need all your papers, needle, thread, bone folder, ruler, pencil and awl. Before you begin, make sure your paper is short grain and your endpapers need to be the same size as the paper you have for your book block.

1. Take your endpapers and put them pattern side to pattern side. If your paper has a specific pattern make sure it matches.

2. Put them on top of the plain papers in your pile.

3. Take your paper for the book block and knock it all up so it is all aligned (in the way news presenters used to shuffle their papers at the end of a bulletin).

4. With your endpapers on the outside of the fold, you need to carefully fold your book block. DO NOT lay the paper down and fold it in half – you will find that one side stays level and the other makes a triangle shape. What you want to aim for is an equal triangle shape, so that both sides move. The easiest way to do this is to hold the paper in the curve of your dominant hand and squeeze in with your fingers very gently – you will start to see the triangle shape appear.

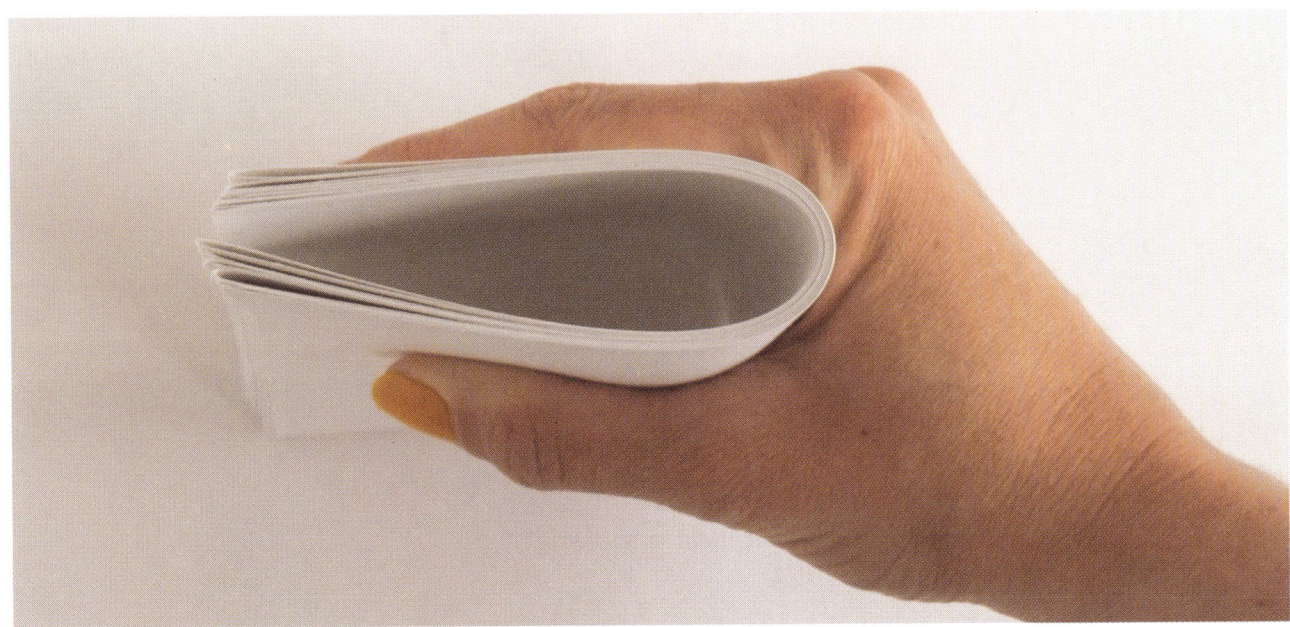

5. You can manipulate the shape using your other hand until you make an even triangle. When you are happy with the shape of your fore-edge you can press the spine edge. Use your bone folder to do this.

6. So now on to sewing: the three holes for sewing need to be evenly spaced out – for example, my paper is 160mm high, my holes are 40mm, 80mm and 120mm. Lightly mark up these points at the fold on the inside of your book block, using a pencil.

7. Using your awl, make holes through your paper at these points. The holes need to go as straight through as you can, do not go in at an angle, and they need to go through the creased spine.

8. Next you will need to thread your needle using bookbinding linen. This is stronger than embroidery thread and is less likely to break. To make life easier for yourself, I recommend 'locking' your needle to the thread. This is fairly easy to do, albeit quite fiddly. The illustrations below will help:

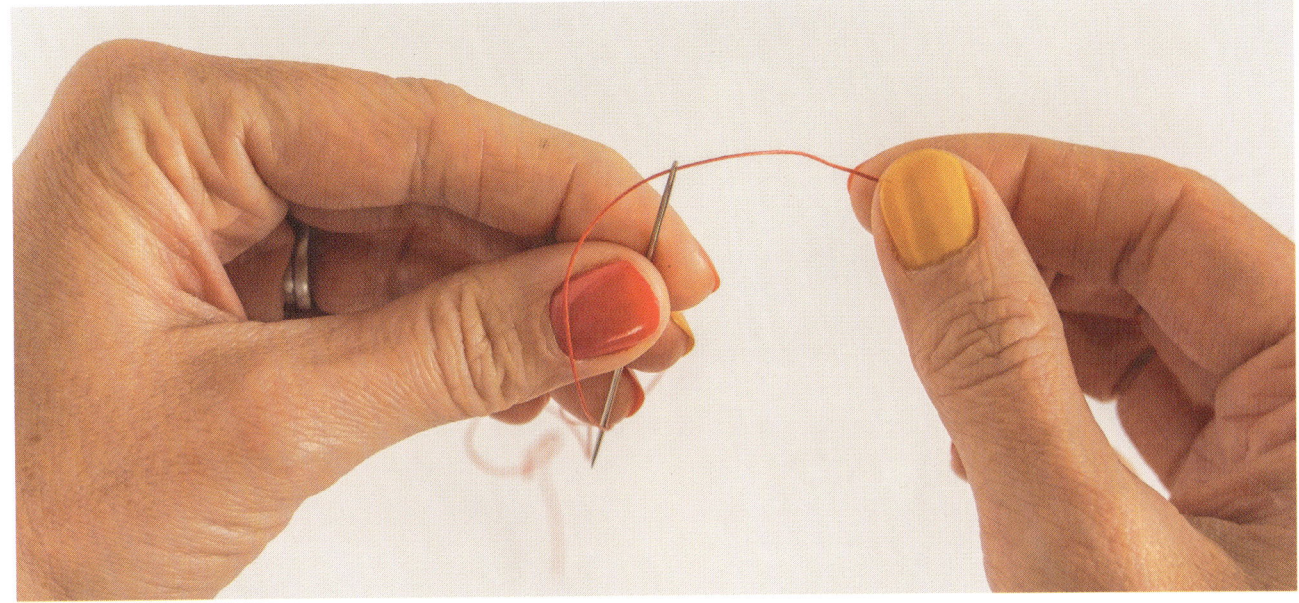

i) Thread your needle leaving about 200mm on the 'short' side.

ii) Take your needle and push it through the thread. It needs to go right through the thread.

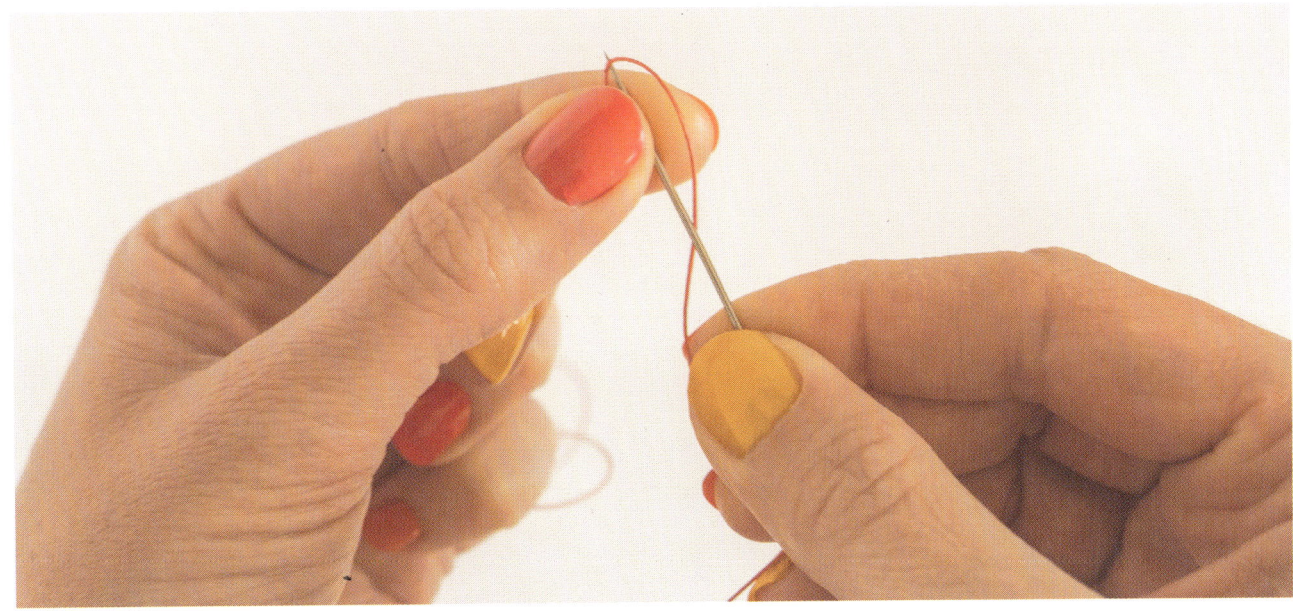

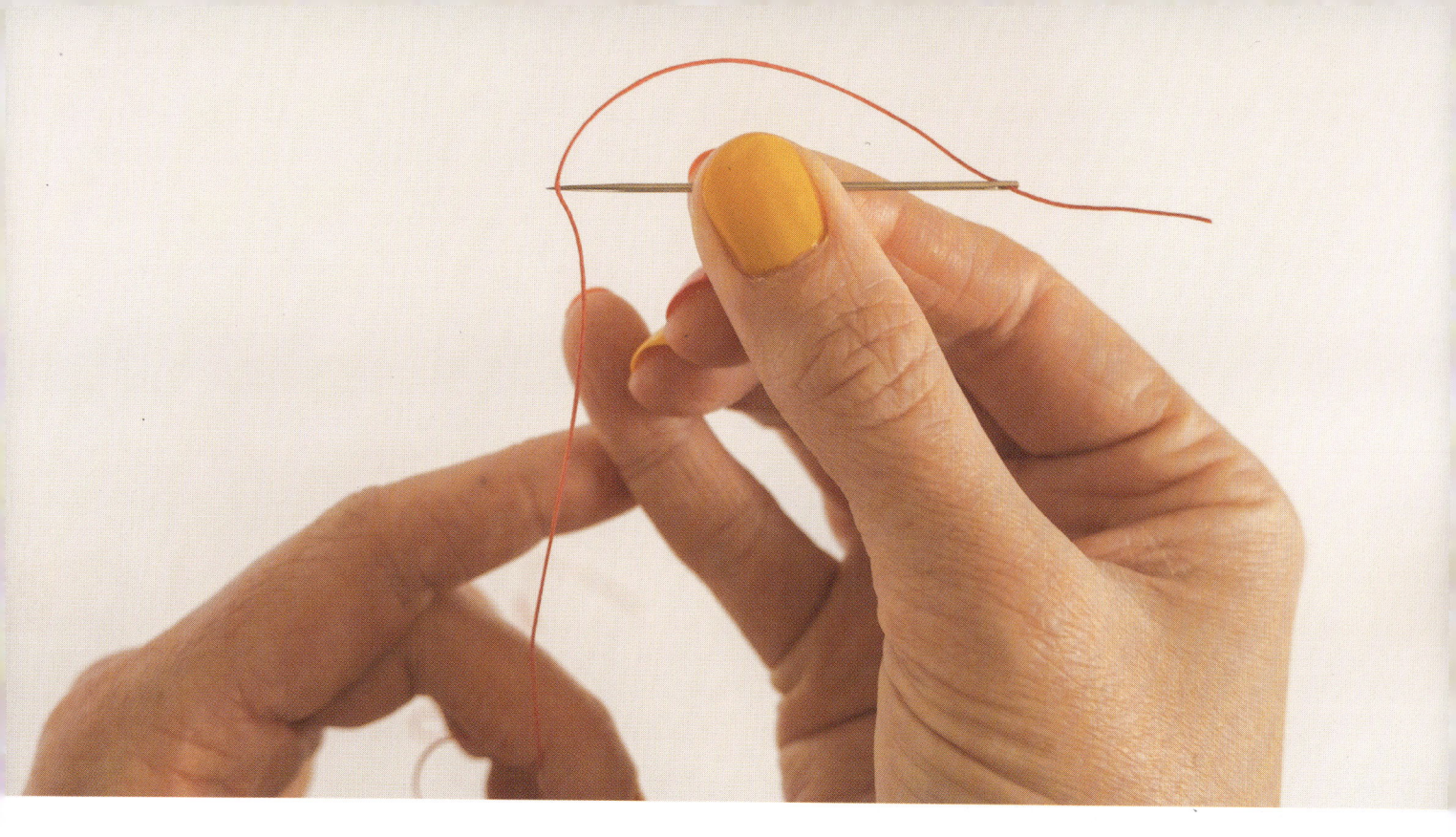

iii) Pull your needle all the way through so you have a D-shape.

iv) Now pull the 'short' side tightly and you will see the thread lock over the needle.

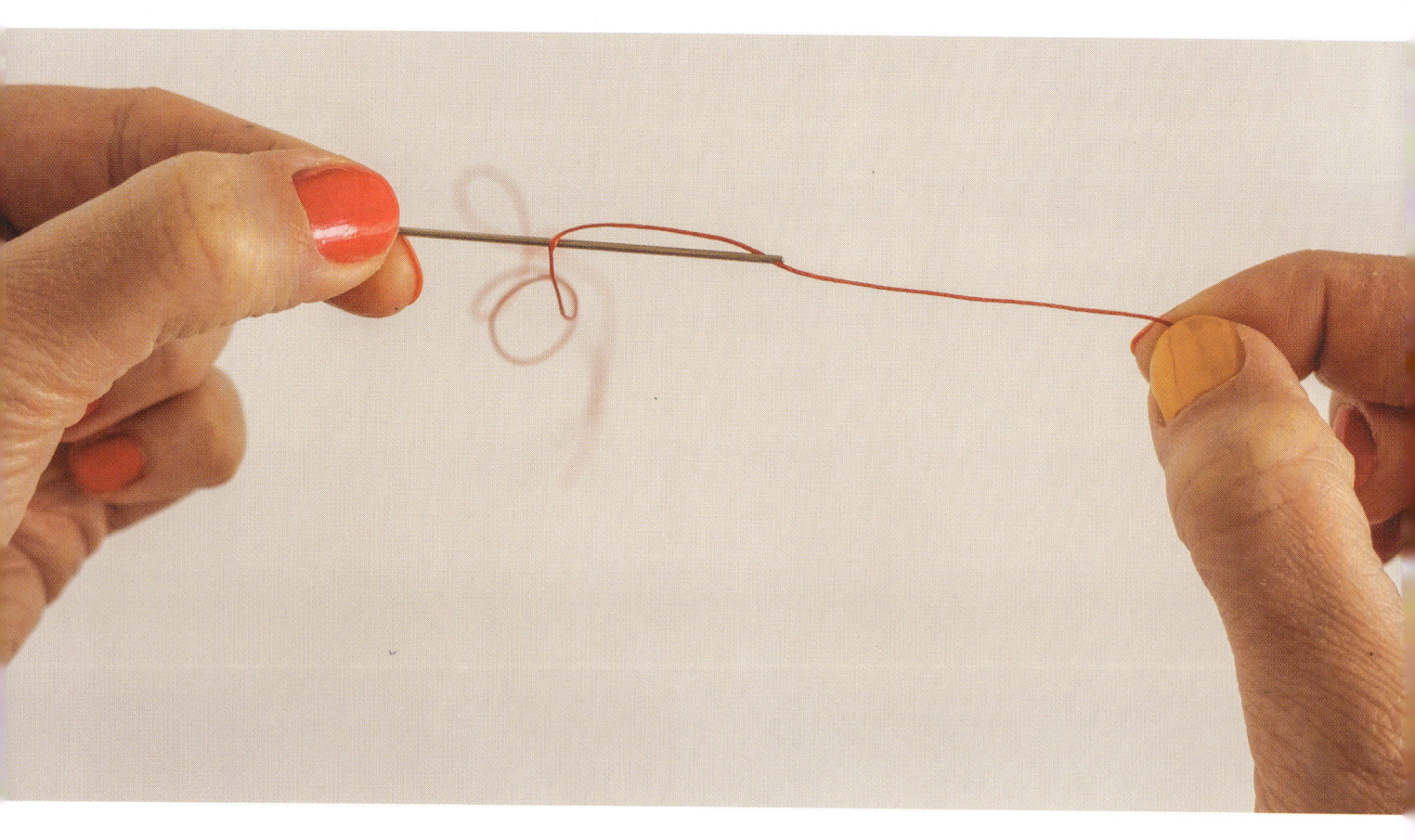

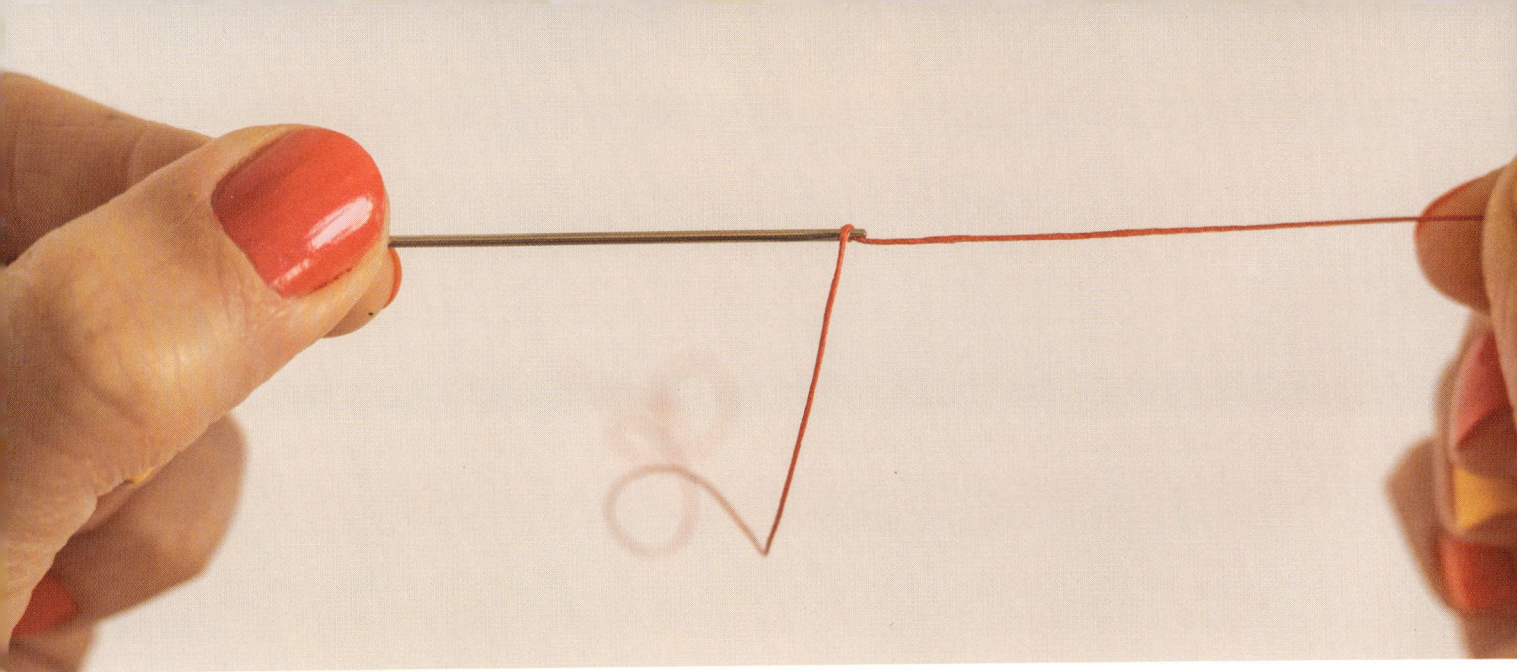

9. Now to sew. This is a three-hole pamphlet binding, however, you can go up to five holes for larger books (see the end of this chapter). What you are aiming for is tight sewing, you do not want baggy thread so make sure you pull tightly at each stage:

i) Starting on the inside of your book block push the needle out through the middle hole and pull until you have 200mm thread left.

Pamphlet Binding

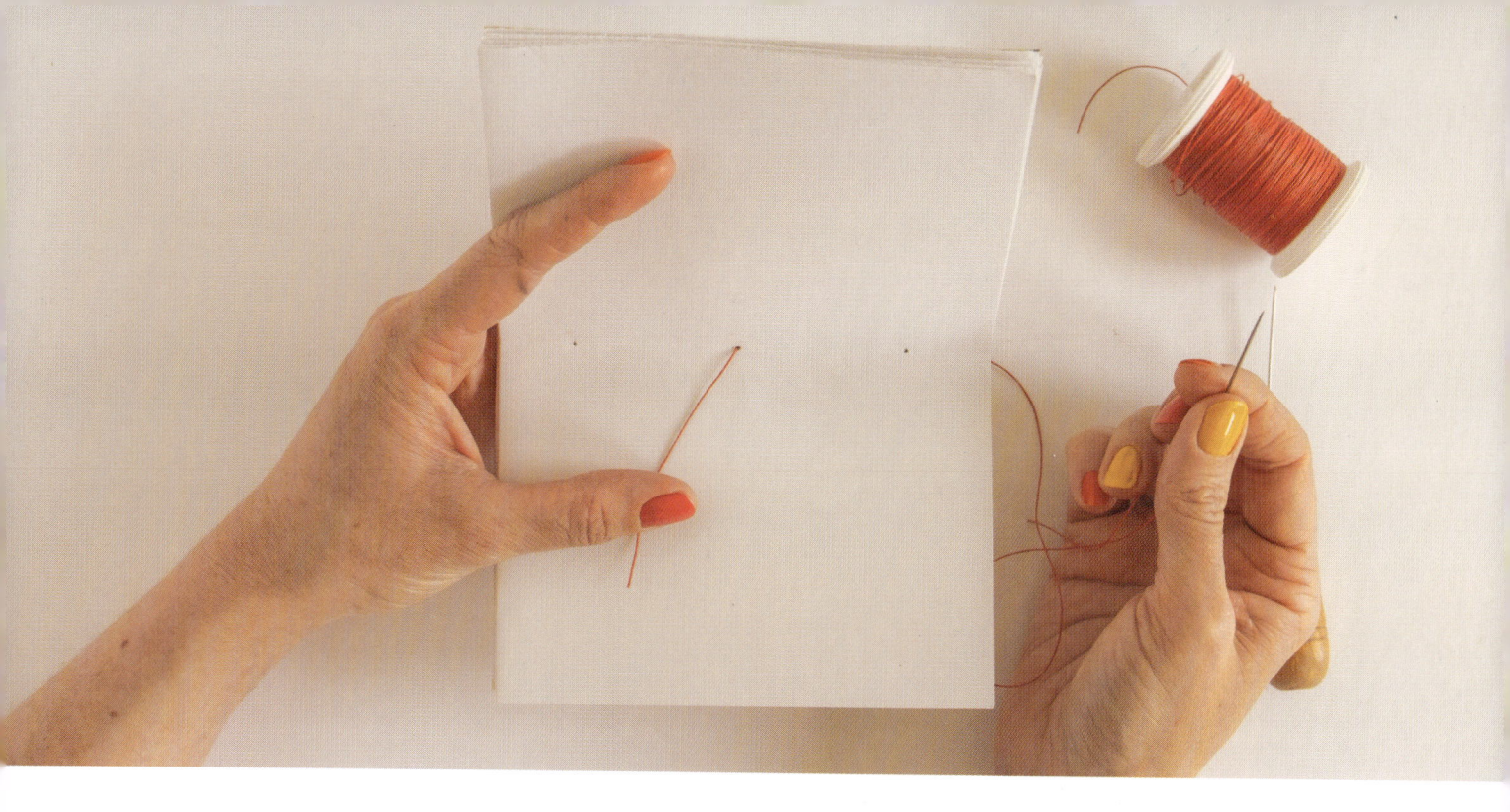

ii) Go to the hole on your left and push the needle back into the centre of your book block.

iii) Cross over the middle and go back out through the hole on the right. Now all of the holes have thread going through them and you are on the outside of your book block.

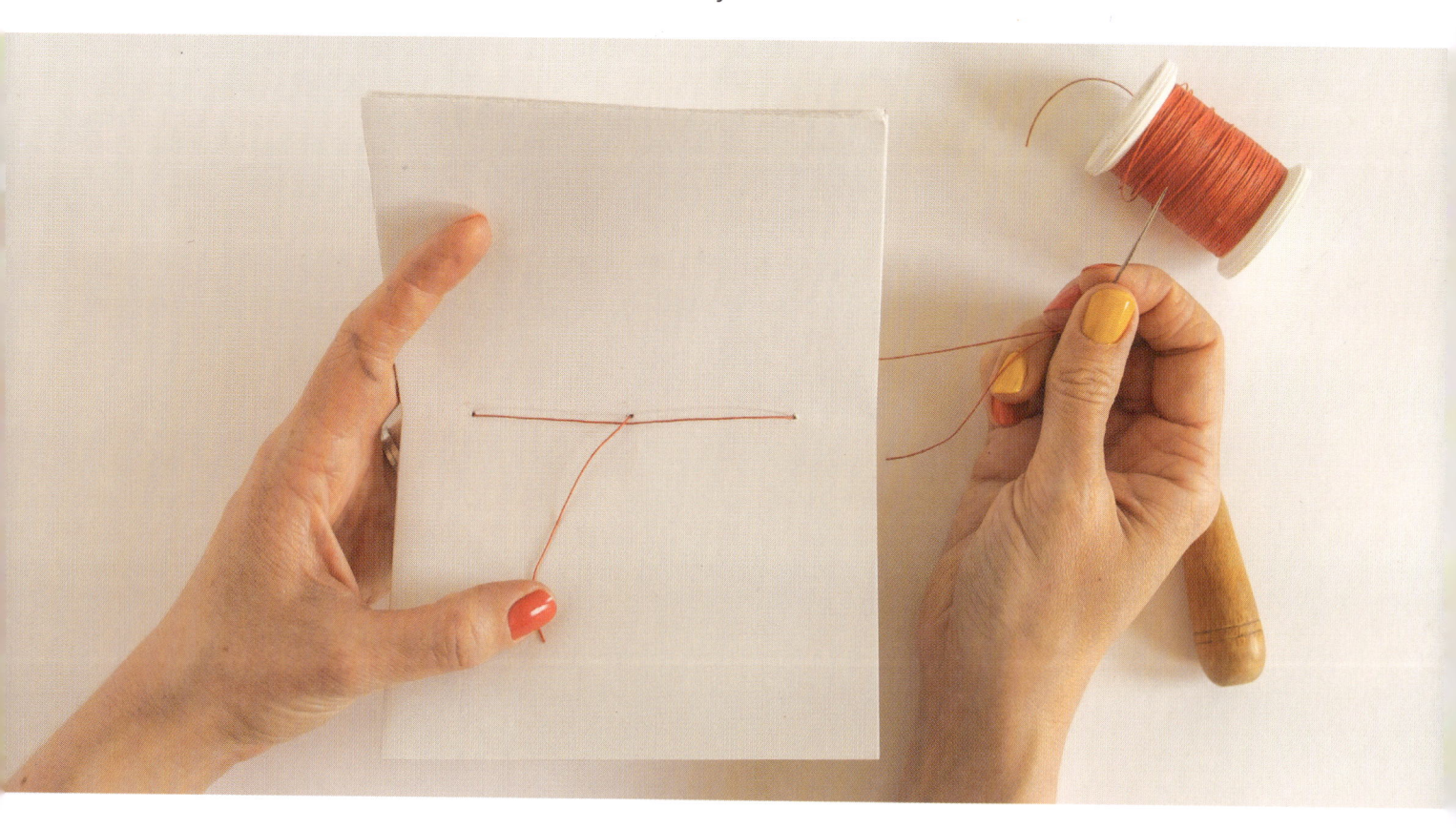

iv) Next you need to go back through the middle hole into the centre of your book. At this point try to make sure you do not pierce the thread already there, and when your needle comes out make sure the 200mm from before and the working thread are on different sides of the thread crossing over the middle.

v) Pull tightly in the direction of sewing (from head to tail, not left to right). Make a double knot once you are happy with the tension – if you give your long thread a flick it should make a twang sound, if not it is all too loose.

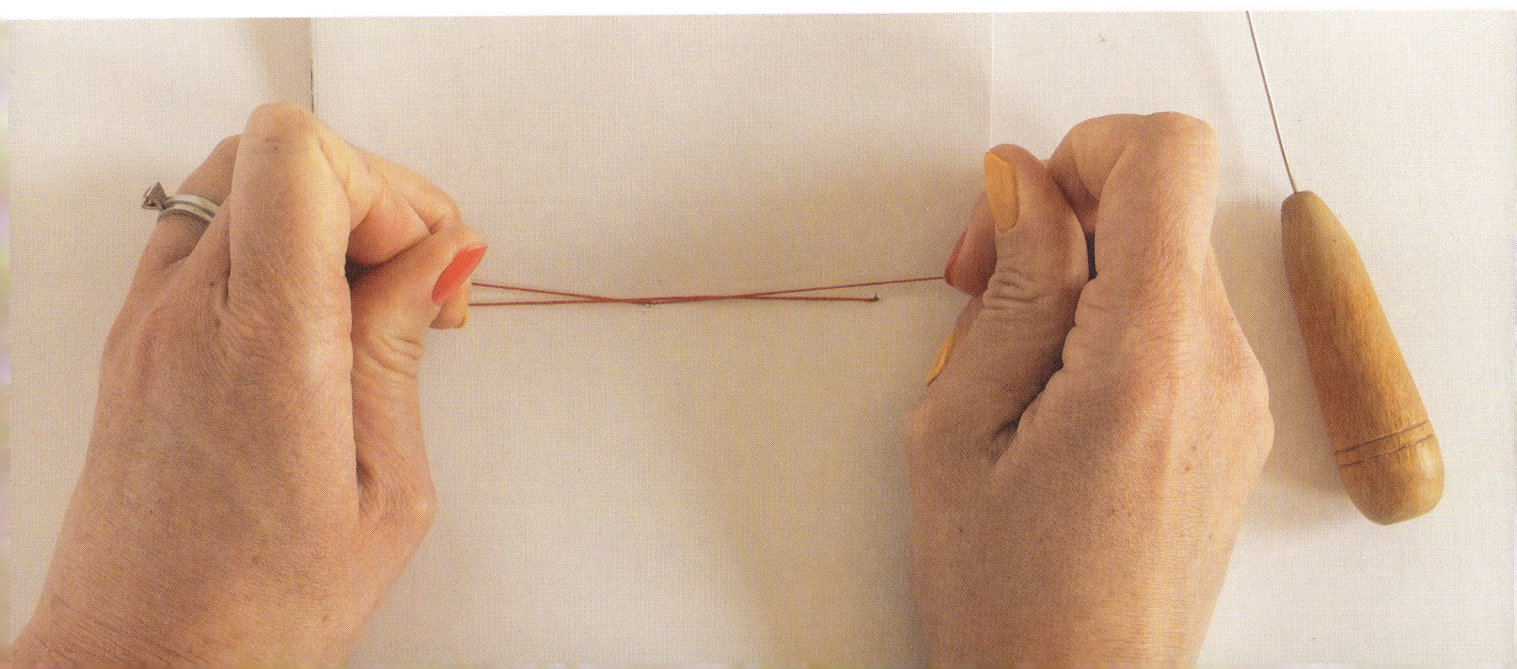

vi) Cut your thread about 15mm from the knot.

At this point you could stop; it is good practice to do this stage a few times so you get used to the sewing method. It is a good way to tidy up loose scrap bits of paper if you are in an office, and it makes an excellent notebook for your bag. You could just use card instead of endpapers and have a slightly sturdier book.

(Please note, this is the point you need to start from when you do the five-hole pamphlet stitch later on in this chapter).

We will now move on to the case:

First you need to cut your grey boards; you need to end up with two cut boards. For this case you will have a big gap between your boards where the spine is. To get the correct measurements for your boards you will need to measure the height of your book block and add 6mm. Now measure the width of your book, so from the spine to the very tip of the triangle at the fore-edge. Take this measurement and subtract 5mm. Cut your grey boards out ready to use. For example, my book is 150mm x 107mm so my boards end up 156mm x 102mm.

a) To measure the gap for your spine, take your book block and place it on one of your cut boards. There needs to be a 3mm square around the book block and the edge of the board – so 3mm at the head, tail and fore-edge (the spine will be further in, do not worry, this is how it is meant to be). Place your other board on top, lining it up on the head, tail and fore-edge; this is easily done by using the edge of your ruler.

b) Now you need the rectangle of paper listed in your materials at the beginning of the chapter. Place it between the book block and the boards on both sides, wrapping it around the spine. Mark the edge of the boards on the paper.

c) Take the piece of paper and measure the space BETWEEN the two lines you have just drawn and add 4mm (this is to allow for the bulk of the boards). My gap is typically around 18mm, so by adding the 4mm I always have around 22mm as my gap size. Write your measurement down on your waste paper or one of the boards (lightly). This size varies from person to person, it depends on what your fore-edge looks like and how hard you pressed your paper as well.

d) Put your block to one side, preferably under a few books to give it a press.

Now to make the case:

e) Your material needs to be around 25mm longer at the head and tail of your boards. For the width, place one of your boards on the back side of the material 25mm from the edge of the fabric, and draw around the board. Now measure your gap (so in this case it is 22mm for me), and then place your other board on the material. Cut the material 25mm away from the edge of your board, and you now have your material with an even turn in.

f) To start, glue up one of your boards with big even circles making sure to cover the board evenly in PVA. Stick the board in the rectangle you just made on your material.

g) Place your ruler along the bottom of your board so it can help to keep the second board in line.

h) Glue up your second board the same way and place it on the material. Measure the distance you made again and make sure it is even all the way along the spine.

i) Turn it over and give it a good rub down with either your bone folder or the heel of your hand.

j) The corners now need to be trimmed as you need to remove some of the excess material.

k) First measure out 4mm from the tip of your corner, this allows for a little bit of a turn in to cover all of the corner. Whatever you do, do not cut flush to the board, you need this little bit of material to cover the corner. If you can, try it on a scrap piece of board and material and see what happens when you do cut flush to the board.

l) I just cut my corners by eye but I have done an awful lot of them, so for now, until you get more confident, measure and cut your corner so you end up with this:

m) Glueing up: glue one of the long edges of the material, be careful to make this an even amount. The perfect amount comes from practice, don't use too much but make sure you get PVA on all of the material. You now need to fold the material over and stick it to the board; make sure you stick it to the edge of the board as well as the part facing you.

n) To make sure you get the material up and on to the side of the board, use the flatter side of your bone folder and place it under the material, then run it along the edge of your board. You will see the material fold up and stick to the board and once you have done this a few times bring your bone folder up and pull the material over the edge of the board. You want to keep doing this all the way along so that the material and the board have no gaps (you do not want air bubbles). Keep working along the material until you are satisfied with what you have done.

o) You will need to swipe and wipe at this stage! You will have some glue come out from the material and go on your bone folder. Swipe the glue off the material with your bone folder and then wipe the bone folder (I wipe mine on my apron, but you can use a cloth). REPEAT FOR THE OTHER SIDE.

p) Now the short edges: you need to pinch in the corners using your index finger nails, then fold the small amount of material you have left on the corner around the edge of the board.

q) Glue up and stick it down using the same method as the longer edges.

r) Then you need to line the sewing on your book block to make sure it is firmly in place and makes your sewing tighter. So cut yourself a piece of paper that is 20mm wide and 10mm shorter than your book block. This also needs to be in the correct grain direction, so the long grain goes head to tail.

s) Glue up the paper with PVA and stick it on to your spine, making sure it is as even as you can get it on both sides and at the head and tail. Make sure you rub it down thoroughly so that there aren't any air bubbles and the paper is stuck firmly to the book, this is so the sewing is covered and this makes it stronger.

t) Sticking your book in: the main thing to remember here is to be brave but also do not look until it is dry! Pop your book block on one of your boards and make sure there is an even gap around the edge of the book and the boards (to form the 3mm square), then place it on your working area.

u) Next glue up your endpapers, go all the way to the edges and down to the spine.

v) Now close the book, make sure you line up the corners of the boards by looking down on your book, and press. Lean on the book for a few minutes

w) Score along the spine next to the board with your bone folder to get the material to stick to the paper. Turn it over and do the other side.

x) And you have done it! Try not to look inside your book for at least four hours and leave it under as much flat weight as you can!

CONGRATULATIONS!! Give yourself a round of applause!!!

So now you have your own notebook. If you have made one before, what went better this time? How can you improve for the next one and what areas do you need to remember to take more care over? What parts do you love and will show off as much as you can?

As I mentioned earlier, you can also do a five-hole pamphlet stitch, which is great for large books or just taller, skinnier books, (I use it to make a lot of list books). This method is better for books larger than A6 in height.

FIVE-HOLE PAMPHLET SEWN BOOK

To make your five-hole pamphlet book the process is the same as above, it is only the sewing that changes and you need to make five holes instead of three.

1. Measure up your paper as before, divide it into 5 and mark the points on the joint again.

2. Make the holes using your awl and we shall begin.

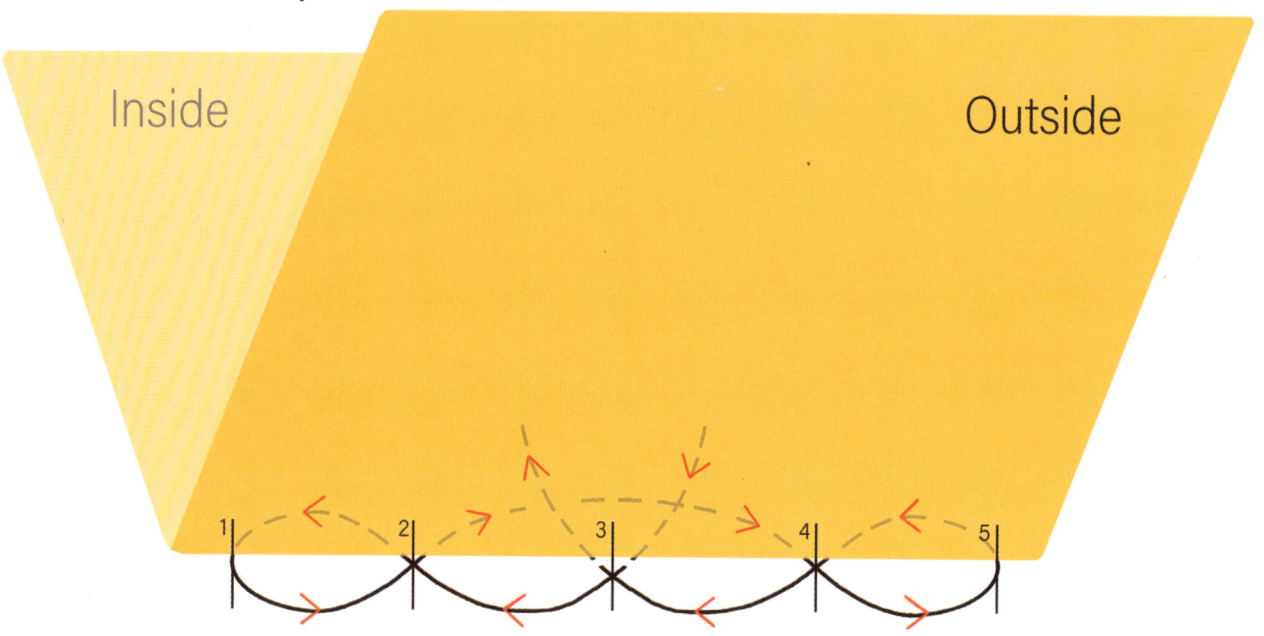

3. Please refer to the handy diagram I have drawn for you as the five holes can get very wordy.

   i) Start at the middle hole (hole three) and push the needle through to the outside leaving a 200mm tail, as with the three-hole pamphlet.

   ii) Now go back inside at hole two and back out of the book at hole one.

   iii) Now go back inside the book at hole two, making sure not to pierce the thread already there.

   iv) Go back outside the book at hole four.

   v) Go back inside at hole five and back out at hole four, making sure not to pierce the thread.

vi) Now all the holes should have been used, pull the thread tightly and go back inside the book at the central hole (hole three). Remember, do not pierce the thread.

vii) Your needle needs to come out the other side of the long thread as you did on the three-hole pamphlet, this is so when you make the double knot to finish the knot does not disappear out of the book.

4. Now you can finish the book in exactly the same way, just take into account the larger boards and material needed. You need to pick up from point a) on page 26 in the three-hole method.

There are a few options of covering in this method of bookbinding: the full cloth as you have just done, or you can also cover them with half bindings and quarter bindings. This means either both the spine and corners are covered in material (half) or just the spine (quarter).

1. Prepare your book block as you have done for the full cloth binding. Once you have it ready, cut your boards in the same way.

2. Take one of your boards and divide the width by four – so if your board is 200mm it will be 50mm in each quarter. This means, in this case, the spine covering will come on to the boards by 50mm, yours will be whatever your board measures out to.

3. Mark this measurement on each board, on both sides, with a line so you know where to stick your material up to.

4. For your corners you need to measure in at a 45-degree angle from the tip of the corner; the same measurement as your spine.

5. Make sure you do it this way, NOT by measuring along the length of your boards.

6. So both boards are now marked up for half binding (your quarter binding will be just the spine).

7. It is easier to cover your corners first with the half binding as you can handle your boards separately.

8. Corners:

   a) Choose your material(s), they can all be the same colour or your corners could be a different colour to your spine.

   b) To measure your material for the corners, make a straight line cut on your material, and place your corners along this line, so the line you have drawn goes along the cut.

Pamphlet Binding • 37

c) Now measure around your board 25mm and cut out four triangles.

d) Glue up and work on each corner one at a time. Glue up the first corner and place it on your board, making sure it lines up with your drawn line. Now cut the corner as you have done with your other covering and turn in the same – so do the head/tail side first and then the fore-edge. Remember to pinch in the corners and then rub down. REPEAT FOR ALL FOUR CORNERS.

9. Now you have your corners covered.

10. Now for measuring your spine gap: this is the same process you used for the full cloth covering. Take your book block and place it on one of your boards; there needs to be a 3mm square around the book block, so 3mm between the edge of the board and the block on the head, tail and fore-edge. Place your other board on top, lining it up on the head, tail and fore-edge.

11. Place the rectangular piece of paper between the book block and the boards on both sides, wrapping it around the spine. Mark the edge of the boards on the paper.

12. Take the piece of paper and measure the space between the two lines you have just drawn and add 4mm.

13. Make sure your material has one straight edge, then place your board along this cut straight edge and make sure your drawn line matches up all the way along. Measure out the gap you just wrote down, so 22mm for me, and place your other board next to this measurement. Now on the material, mark up where the line is on your second board.

14. There needs to be 25mm of material at the head and tail as well. Once you have all of these marked out, cut out your rectangle of material.

15. Now glue up your material, this is a bit different as it is a small piece and it is easier to glue the material than the boards. . Once the material is all glued up, place one board on the material with the line drawn matching along the edge of the material. Then place a ruler along the bottom side of the board and place the other board with the edge of the material, matching the line drawn on the board. Turn over and rub down.

16. Then turn in your head and tail in the same way as you did for the full binding.

17. Next on to the filling: this can be done with either a different colour material or paper. Just remember, if you use paper it needs to be strong (100gsm minimum) and THE CORRECT GRAIN DIRECTION.

18. You will need to end up with two pieces of paper or material like this at the end of this process:

To get to this shape:
   a) Cut the paper/material into a rectangle that is 50mm taller than the boards and the same width – remember turn ins on the three sides.

b) Once you have this, lay the paper (going the correct way) on one side of your boards, make sure it is 2mm over the material on your spine and then fold in the corners so the paper covers 2mm of the corner material as well. This is because you want the paper to go over the edge of the material, not butt up to it directly.

c) Cut the paper/material at the corners so you end up with the shape as seen in the photos on page 41.

d) Mark this paper/material with a star and the side you measured it from with a star as well.

e) Do the same for the other side – MAKING SURE THE PATTERN GOES THE RIGHT WAY TOO!

19. Now glue them up and stick them on. You need to be brave at this point again and work quickly – please read ahead until step 23 so you know what is coming, and what to look out for.

20. To glue up the paper/material, make large circles and glue from the middle out. Your paper is going to curl up but just keep brushing the paper until it stops – this means that the PVA has been absorbed on to the paper enough so it will stretch out properly.

21. Once all glued up, pick your paper/material up and place the long edge on the material 2mm that you measured up. Now lay the paper/material down and shift it until you are happy with where it is on the board. Once you are happy, rub it down with the heel of your hand GENTLY as the paper might be weak as it has been glued out.

22. Next, turn in the edges – it does not matter what order you do this in as there are not any corners to turn in.

23. Then repeat for the other side.

24. And there you have your finished half-bound cover.

25. Stick your book block in the same way as you did for the full binding.

QUARTER BINDING

1. So, you have your spine covered as we did this together for the half binding. Covering the board left exposed is a lot easier for a quarter binding as you have no corners to worry about.

2. Cut out two rectangles of material/paper, 50mm taller and the same width as the boards.

3. Remember to make sure the grain direction is going the correct way and that the pattern is also going the correct way for each piece.

4. Glue up one side and keep brushing out until it stops curling.

5. Pick up your paper with your fingertips – making sure you have the correct long edge along the spine material – and place the paper 2mm over the edge of the material and lay your paper down so there is the 25mm allowance all the way around (roughly).

6. Now rub down with the heel of your hand – being gentle so you do not tear the paper.

7. Next turn over and cut your corners as you have before with the corners of your material – leaving 4mm for covering. At this point you will find it easier to just cut them rather than waiting and measuring them, so be brave!

Pamphlet Binding • 45

8. Work the head and tail first, pinch in the corners and turn in the fore-edge, do the same for the other side.

9. There you have it: a quarter-bound cover.

10. Stick your book block in as with the full cloth binding and admire your work!

That concludes our first venture into bookbinding. How much do you love it? I remember the first books I made, I knew I was hooked and couldn't see myself doing anything else. Going from flat paper to an actual notebook still amazes me even eight years later. I hope you have enjoyed yourself, go ahead and admire your work and be pleased with what you have just done. Now either go back and do it all over again or turn the page and let's begin a new chapter together.

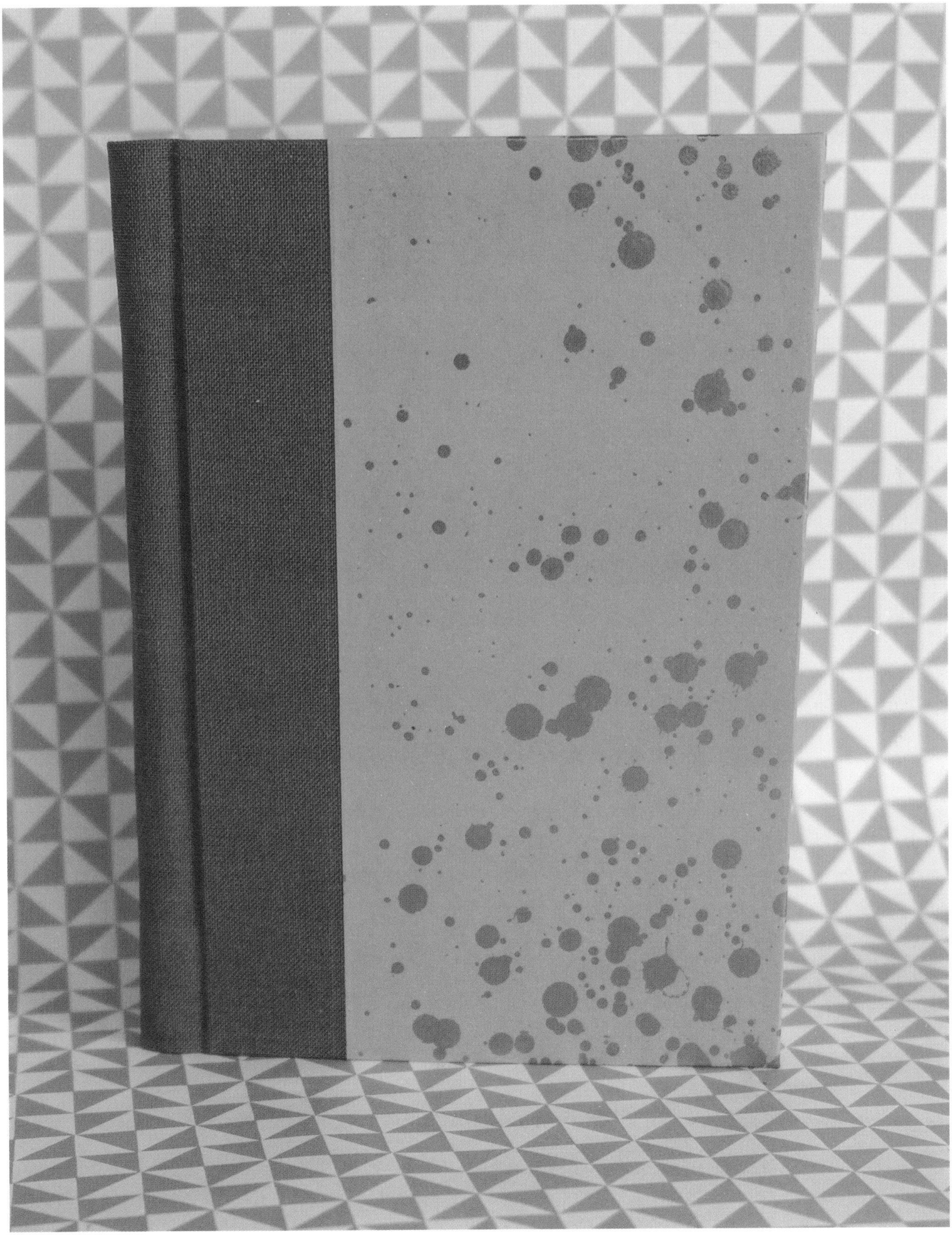

CHAPTER TWO

Intermediate Bookbinding

THIS CHAPTER WILL show you how to make section sewn notebooks. This method is more complicated than the pamphlet notebook from the last chapter, so if you have not tried that I recommend you go back and make the pamphlet-style notebook first as it will get you used to sewing paper and making a case. The main thing to pay attention to with sewn notebooks is the tension in your sewing. The sewing is an integral part of the structure and strength of your book – too loose and it will come apart, too tight and it will be difficult to open your book up flat. The best way to get on top of this is to practise, I recommend you sew a couple of book blocks before you sew one to cover, as you will notice a difference.

Bookbinding is simple once you know how, so do not be put off if you are not happy at first or if it takes a while to do. Take the time, practise what you need and concentrate on the task at hand, trying to give it your full attention. I find sewing book blocks clears my mind and I find it very therapeutic. Be kind to yourself, you are learning and by doing it you will only get better over time.

MAKING A SECTION SEWN NOTEBOOK

For this you will need:

Paper for your book block
Endpapers
Material for covering
Grey boards 2mm
Sewing needle
Thread
Bone Folder

Awl
Beeswax
Ruler
Pencil
PVA
Glue brush
Waste paper
Scissors
Scalpel
Cutting mat
Cord
Kraft paper – brown packing paper for lining your spine
Ribbon

This method of bookbinding is more difficult than the pamphlet binding you have done previously, but it is a professional way of binding a notebook. It yields amazing results and ones you can customise completely. It is important you get the basics down though so try and make sure you sew a few book blocks before moving on to the covering of the book.

Let's start to make your book block:

1. To begin with you will need to have paper that is roughly A4 in size as we will be making an A5 book. Try not to use A4 paper as the grain direction will probably be long grain and you will need your paper to be short grain (so going from head to tail), as this makes it easier to fold and then add your endpapers to later on. Get A3 long grain paper and cut it in half to make A4 short grain paper. (Please see my list of stockists for A4 paper that is specifically created for making books. It is slightly more expensive than cutting down A3, but maybe easier.)

2. Once you have thirty sheets of A4 short grain paper you are ready to get folding.

3. With my books I use 110gsm paper and fold in sections of three sheets, so I get ten sections of three sheets. I do not recommend going above three pages, but you can adjust this if you are using thinner paper, just make sure each section does not go too far above 330gsm (3 x 110gsm).

4. Now to folding: this is the same principle as the single section book you made in Chapter 1. Do not just fold the paper flat on the table, make sure you make the points at the fore-edge meet – it is less pronounced on these sections as it is only three sheets, but it does make a difference. Fold all ten sections.

5. We now need to make a template to make your holes. With this sort of sewing you always need to have an even number of holes (unlike pamphlet binding where you need an uneven number). Make yourself a template from thick paper.

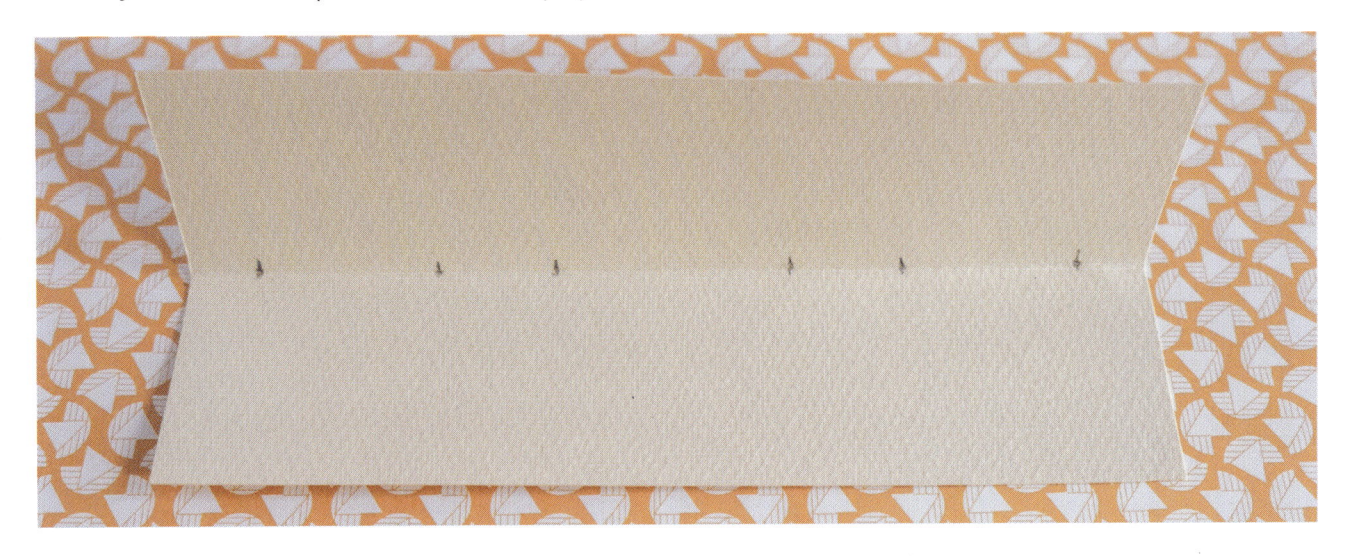

6. The holes need to be evenly spaced. The kettle stitches at the head and tail are the stitches that keep the sections together.

7. Make holes in each section using your awl. As with the pamphlet binding you need to make sure you go through the paper at a 45-degree angle.

8. Now all of your sections have been punctured you should see all of the holes line up. This is a very satisfying process to me. Remember at this stage you can do as many as you want.

9. Your sections now need to be pressed under weights for a few hours so that the 'air' in the folds goes away. Just put your book under a board and either put weights on top or a few hardback books. You'll see the difference:

10. Next we come to sewing: at this stage I recommend reading ahead all the way to stage 32 so you know what to expect and learn any little pitfalls you may fall into.

11. Remember you need for sewing:

> *Needle*
> *Thread*
> *Scissors*
> *Bone folder*
> *Weight*
> *Table*
> *Beeswax*
> *Nerves of steel! Not really, this is easy once you have the hang of it, I promise.*

12. You will need your thread to be approximately six times the length of your book, this is because you want to try and reduce the number of times you need to connect new threads. Once you have your thread you then need to wax it. Most bookbinding thread is unwaxed, and it is OK to leave unwaxed if you are vegan or do not have beeswax, but waxing makes the thread glide through the book more smoothly and makes sewing that little bit easier. Just take your thread in one hand and your beeswax in another and run the thread over the beeswax, then run it through a cloth to remove any excess.

13. This thread is not long enough to do your whole book, do not try and have a piece that is, madness lies there and a lot of knots! This means you will need to join your thread to a new piece at some point, so try to make the join is on the outside of your book by a middle hole, keeping the join away from your kettle stitches.

14. To join the threads you need to do a weaver's knot:

A picture goes with each stage:

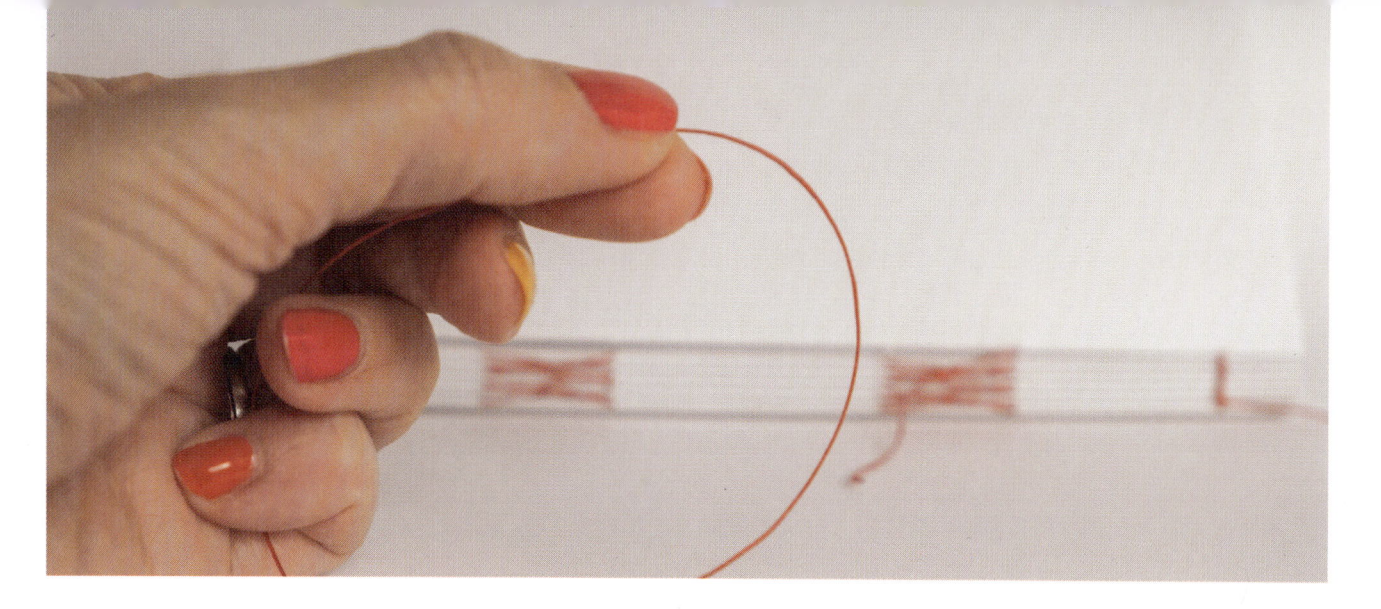

a) Take your new piece of thread and have about 60mm to work with.

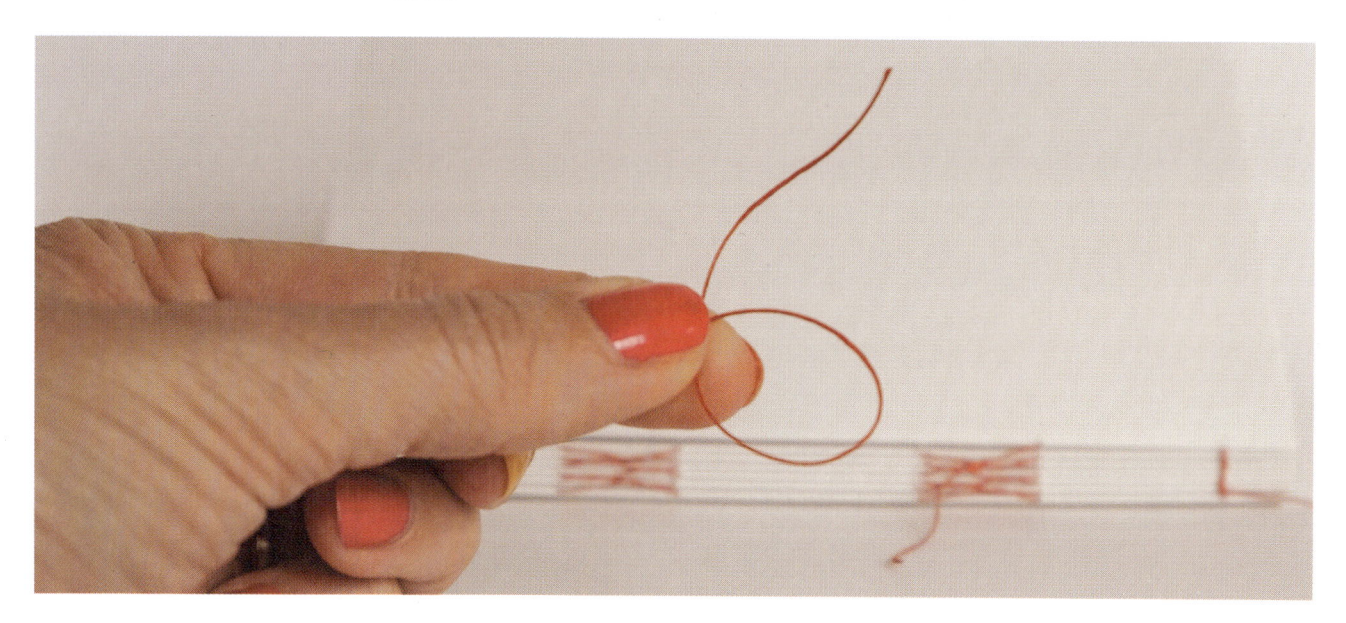

b) Make a loop in the thread by placing the smaller end over the larger end of the thread

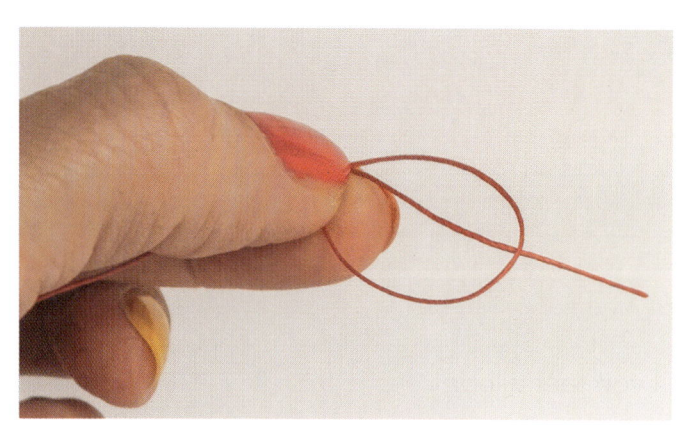

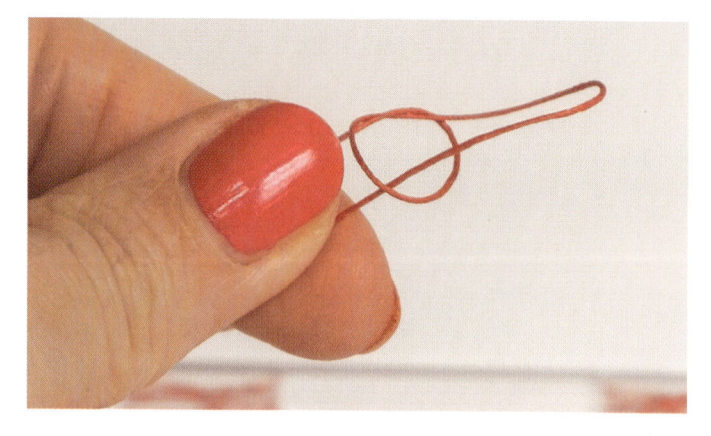

c) Pull part of the smaller thread through the hole to make a loop.

d) Pull the two threads tight.

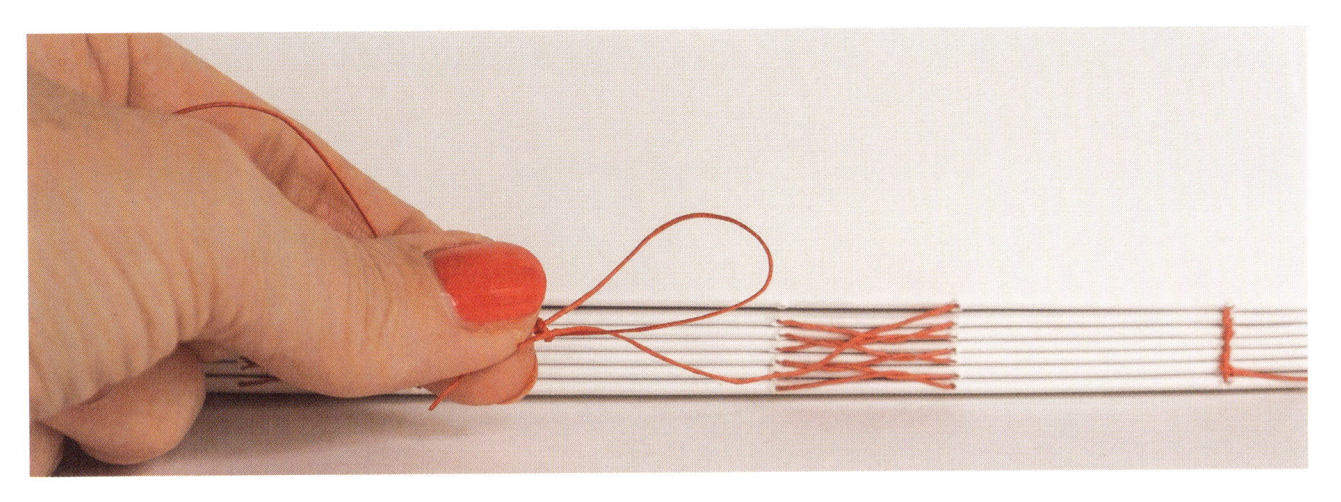

e) Place the loop over the thread left on your book

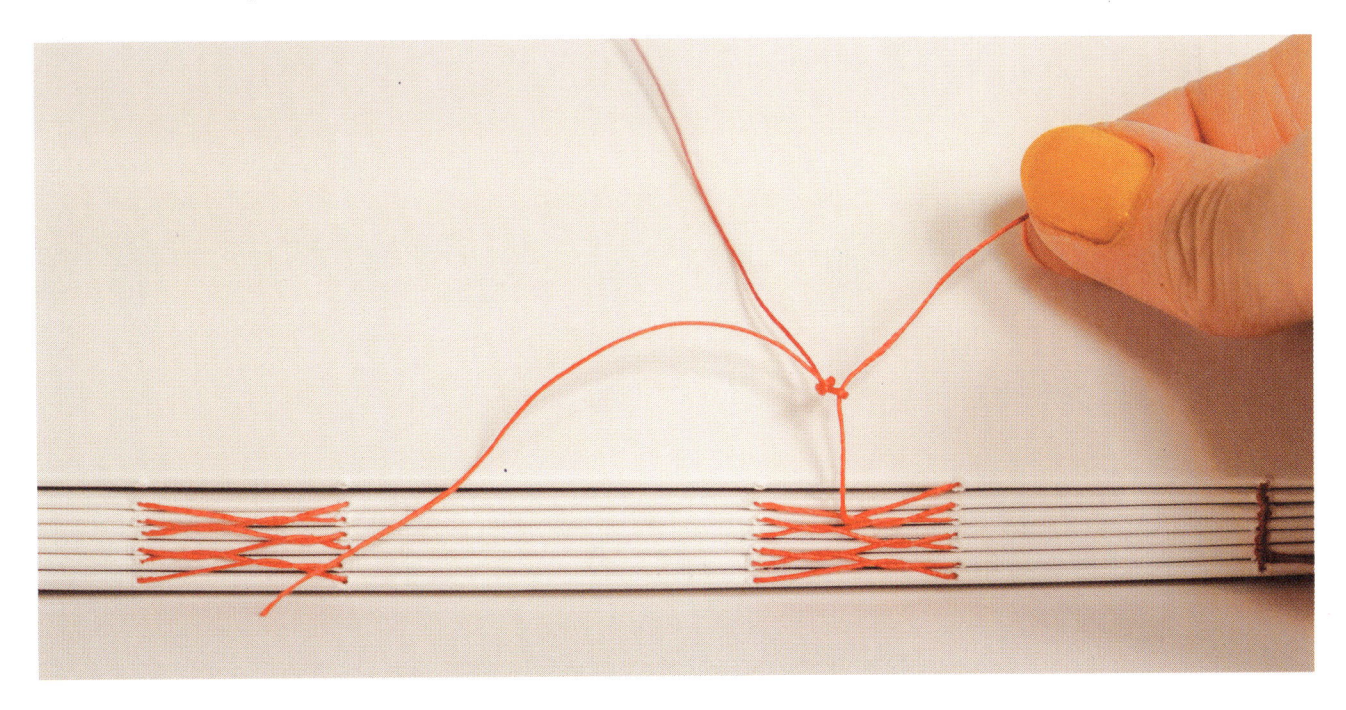

f) Pull the shorter thread of the loop tight until you feel a 'pop'

Intermediate Bookbinding • 55

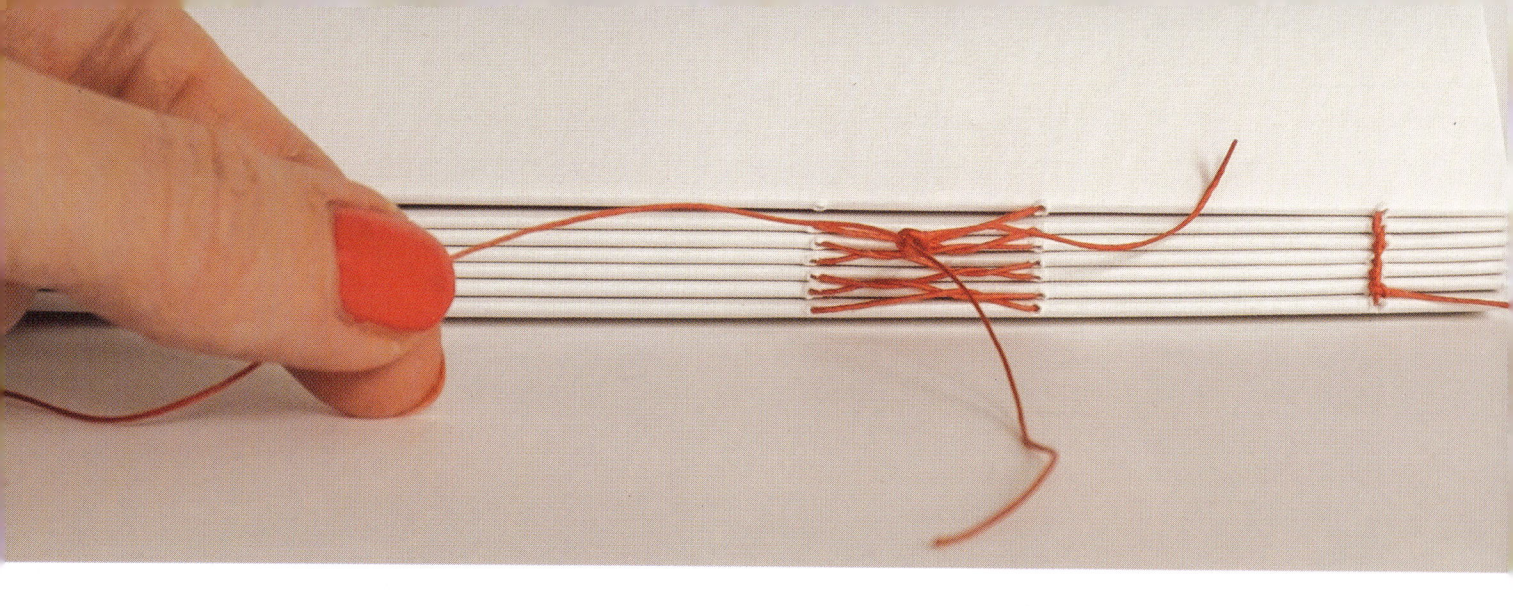

g) Once you have checked the knot has taken you can trim the two shorter pieces of thread, being careful not to cut the longer thread you will be using!

15. Thread your needle and lock the thread on to your needle, as shown in Chapter One.

16. Take one section and place it on the edge of your table with the spine facing you. Starting from the right, go from the outside inside until you have gone along the whole length.

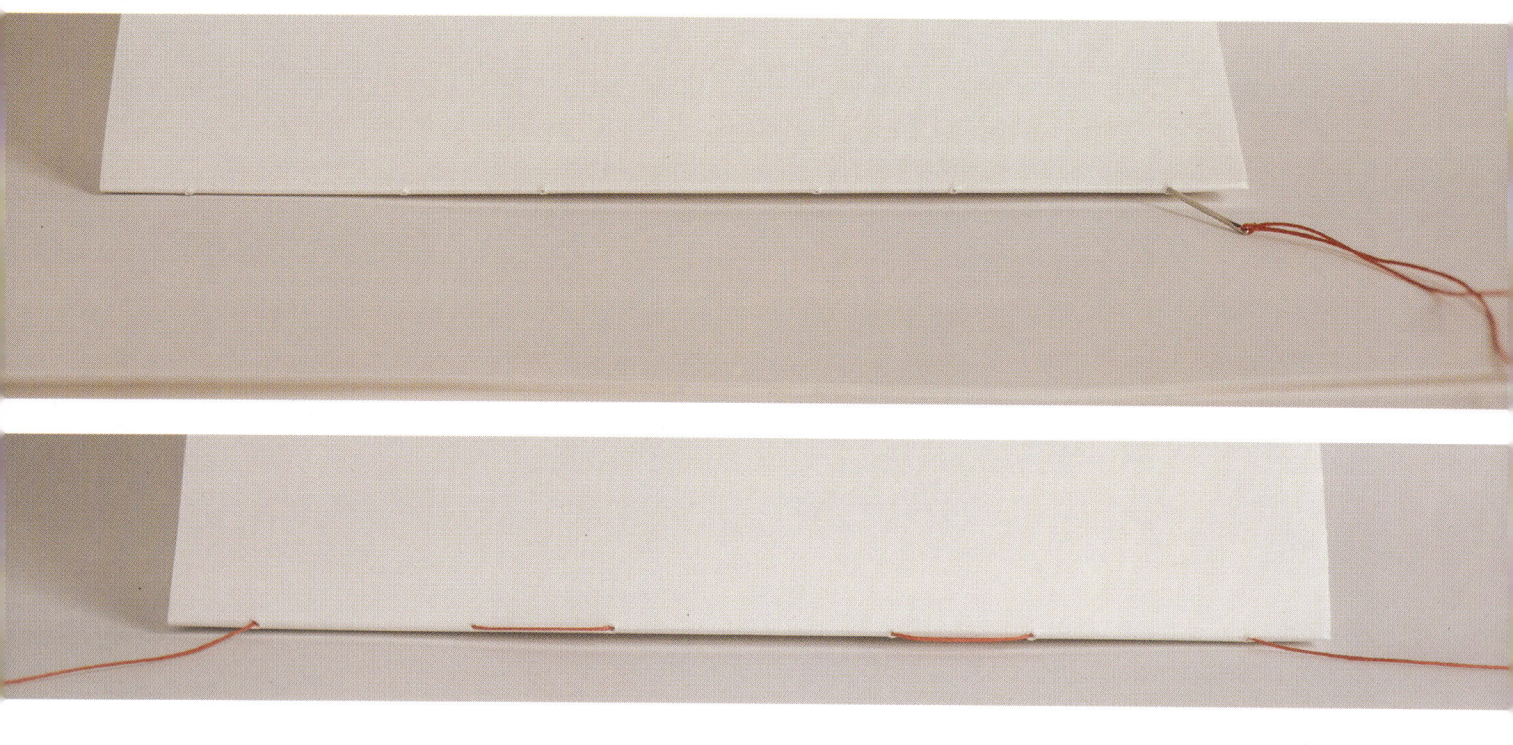

17. Pull the thread tight so you have about 200mm of thread coming out from the hole where you started. Rub down with a bone folder and place section two on top.

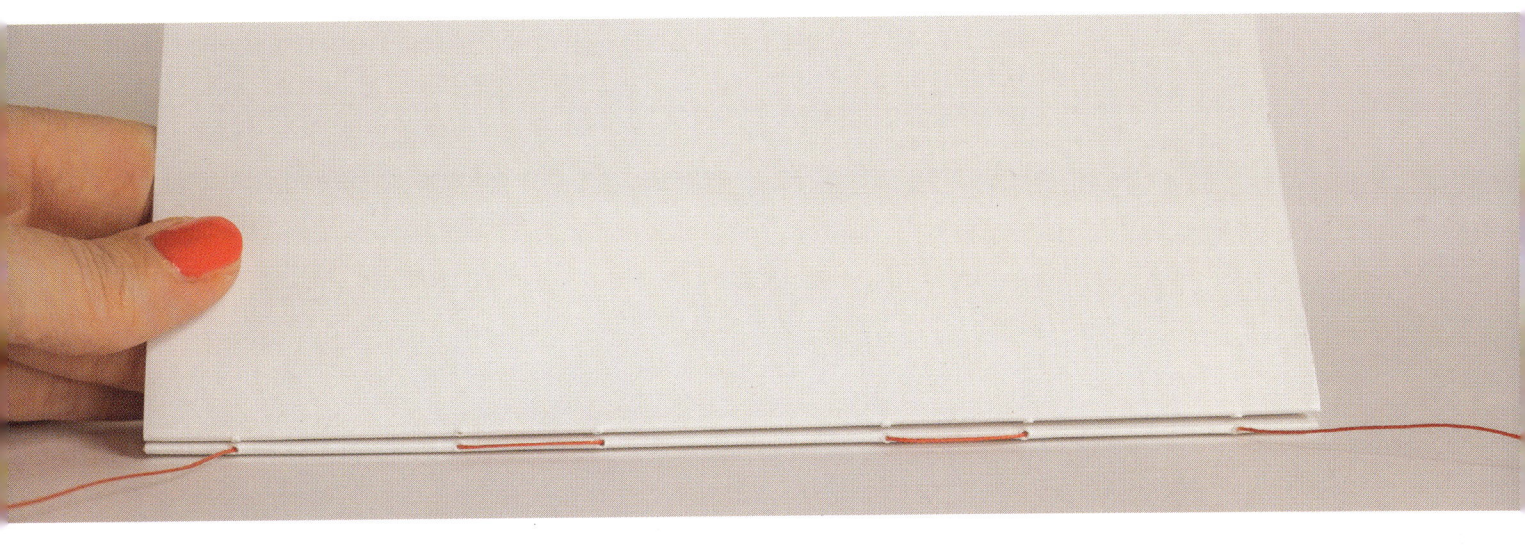

18. Your holes should line up perfectly, as you have made them all with the same template, so all of your edges should line up as well. Put your weight in the centre of your second fold so it stays in place – it is not necessary, but I was trained using weights so now find it hard to sew books without them.

19. First, go up into section two through the kettle stitch and come out at the next hole along.

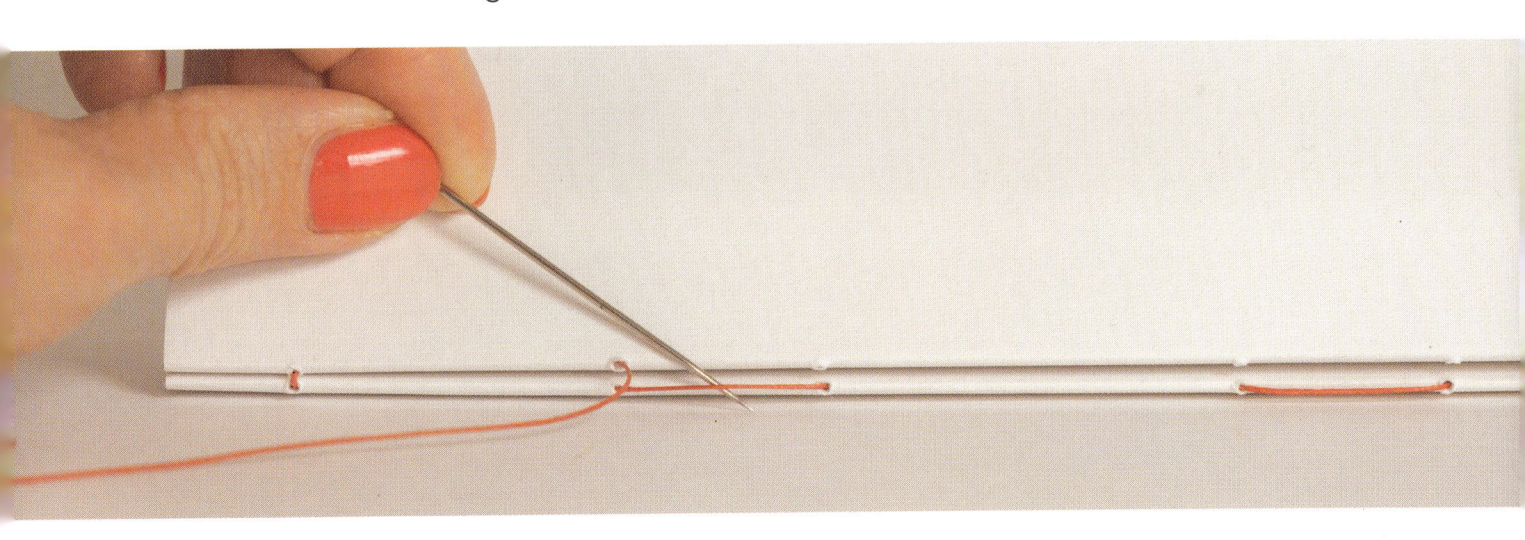

20. Now to hook up with the section below. Put your needle behind the exposed thread and pass it through so you are hooking your working thread with the stitch below it.

21. Go back in through the next hole and come out again and hook up with the stitch below in the same way, and then back in the next hole and out at the kettle stitch.

Intermediate Bookbinding • 57

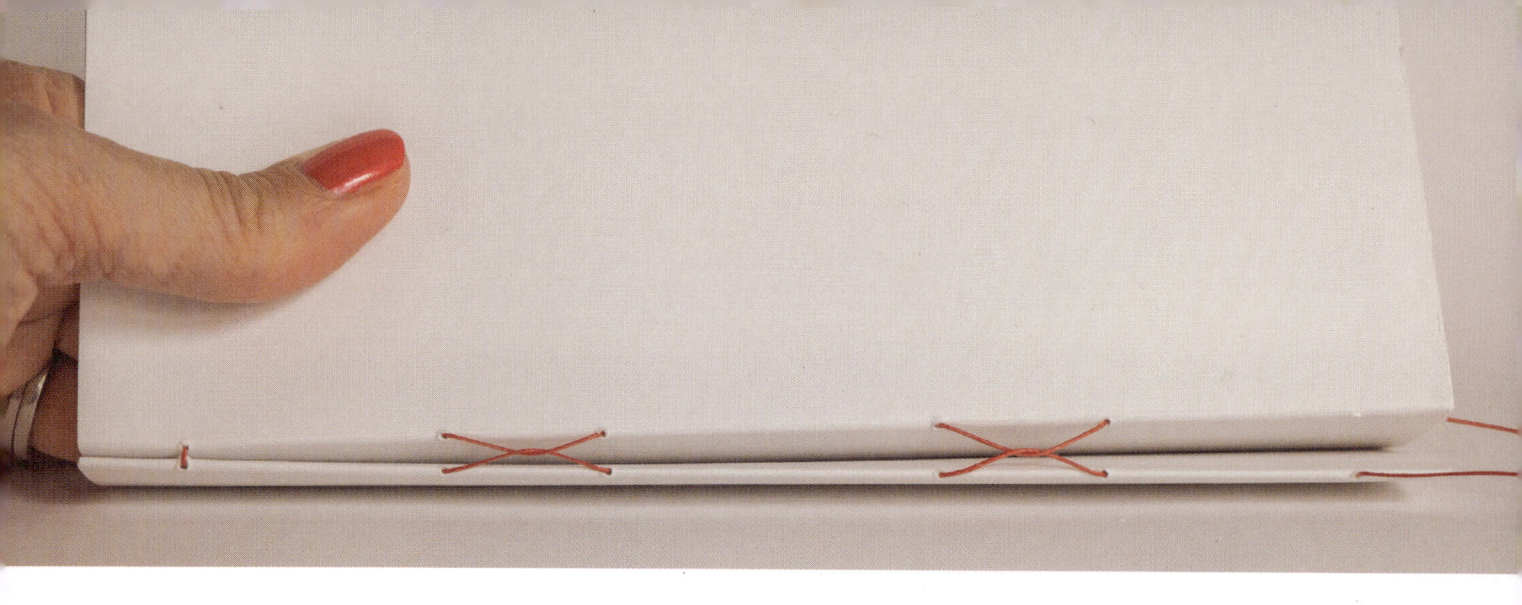

22. Now pull both threads tightly away from your sewing (so pull to the right) and double knot the threads, keeping them as tight as you can. As you progress up this book, and on to others, your tension will get better and be more even, so just allow yourself to practise.

23. Good work so far, so now remove the weight and rub both sections down with your bone folder.

24. Go along the same as section two making sure to hook up the section below. PLEASE NOTE THAT YOU ONLY PICK UP THE THREAD FROM THE PREVIOUS SECTION NOT ALL OF THE SECTIONS

25. Once you have sewn all along pull your thread tight, then you need to link up with the kettle stitch below.

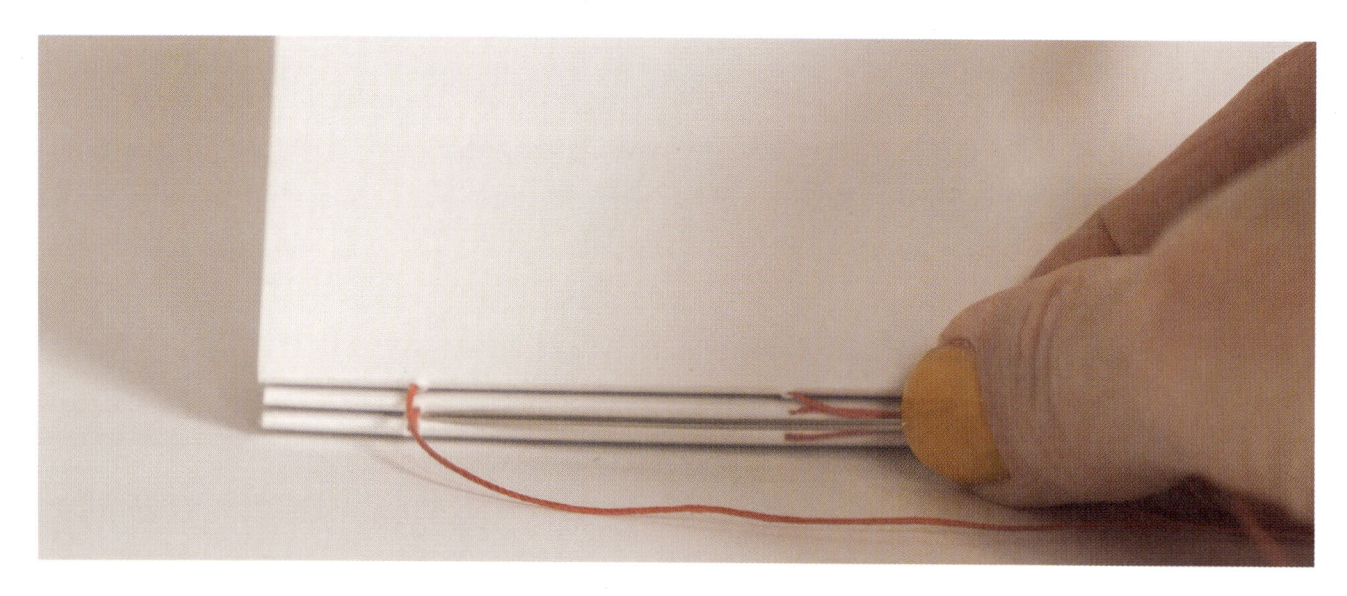

26. Place your needle between the previous two sections in the space between the kettle stitch and the link stitch. Push your needle so you can pull it out at the head/tail.

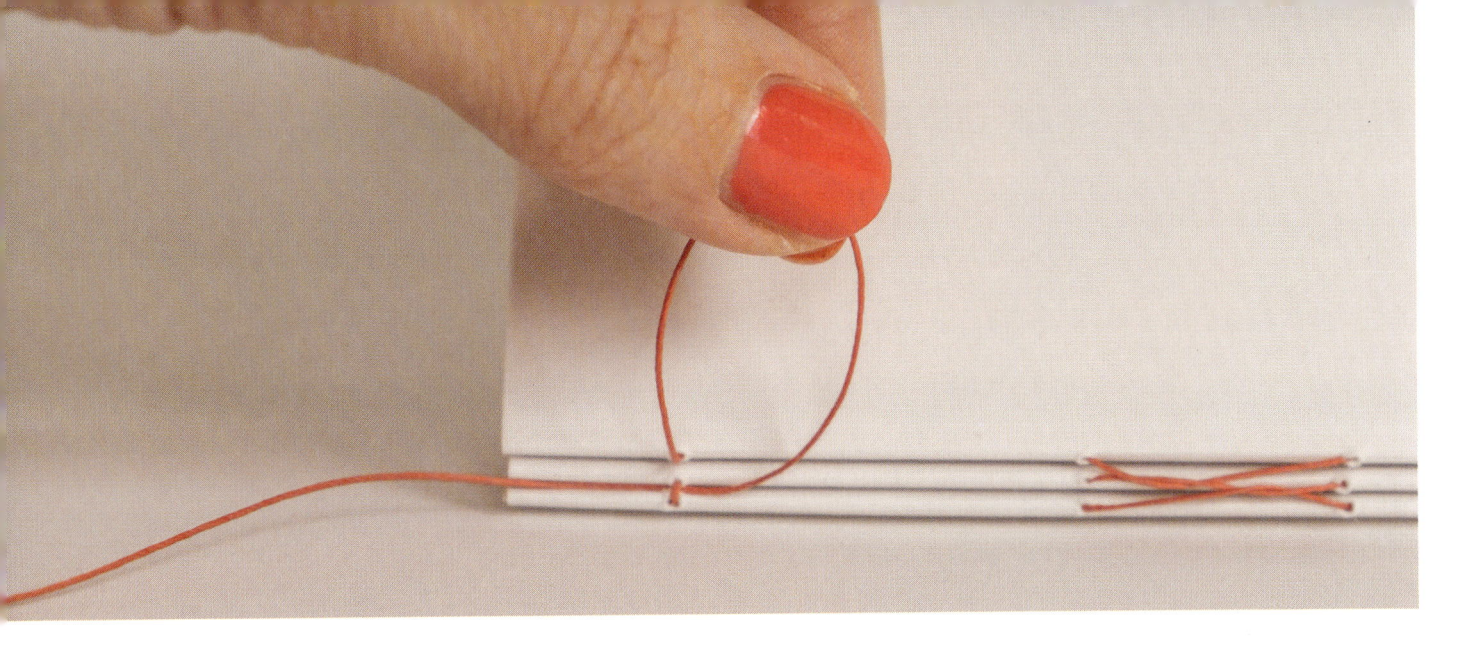

27. Pull through so you get a loop.

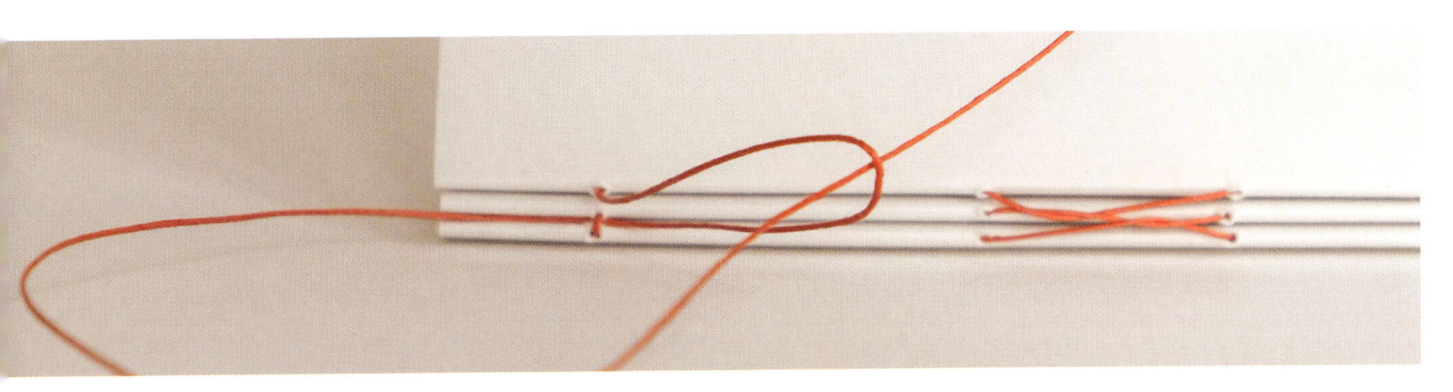

28. Pass your needle and thread through the loop from the bottom up.

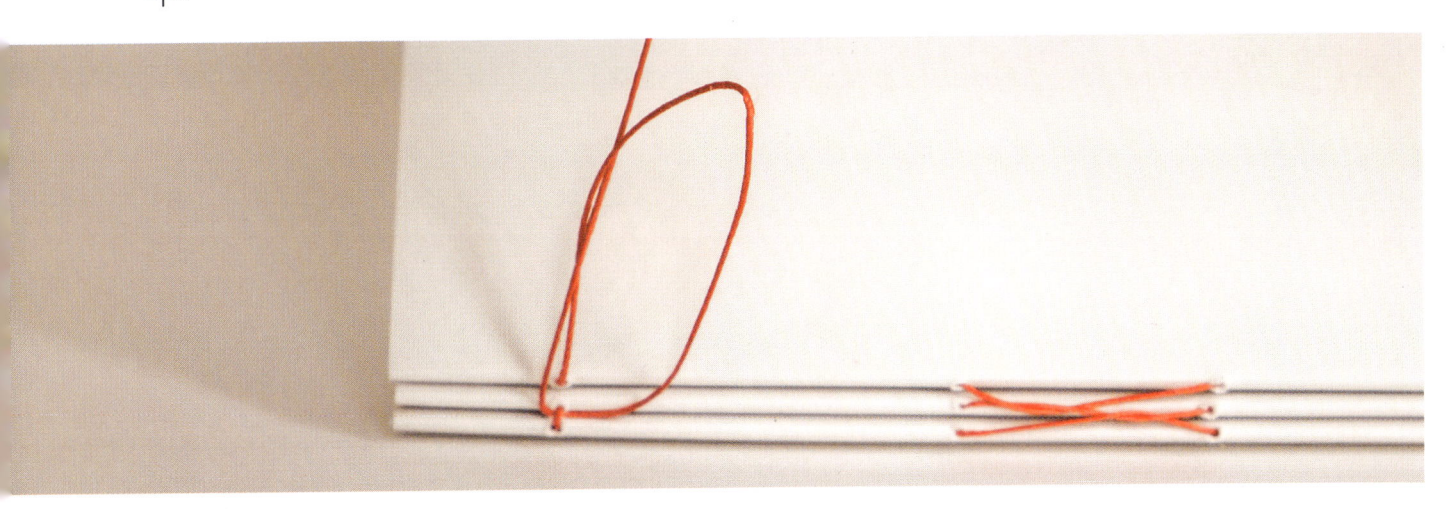

29. Pull the thread coming out of the section you have worked on tight, then pull your needle and thread. All of the thread will come through the loop and pull tight, this makes sure that your thread does not become loose and your sections are really attached to each other.

Intermediate Bookbinding • 59

30. Now keep doing steps 23–29 until you have finished the book. You will probably need to attach the thread a couple of more times before you finish it completely.

31. When you get to the last section, make sure you knot at the kettle stitch twice to make sure it's completely secure.

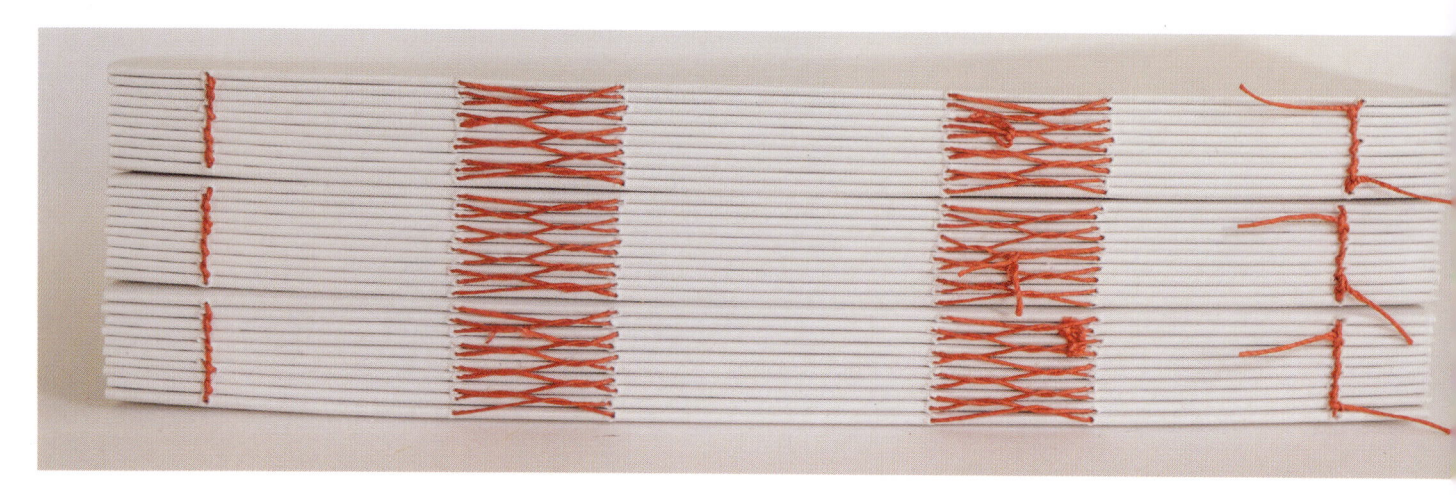

32. Congratulations, you have finished your book. It will still feel a little bit flimsy at this stage, and you will need to glue it up to make it firmer.

At this point I would recommend you sew a few more books up before you go any further. Try to keep track of all your progress and see how much better your sewing becomes. It should always be fairly neat as you have pre-made your holes.

Use the space below to write down what you think went well, and what to keep an eye on next time you sew up. Refer to this every time you sew up a book block so you will get better. Practice makes for progress.

33. Now your book needs to be glued up. Place some scrap paper on the edge of a table where you can leave your book out of the way overnight. You will need some scrap boards for the next part, it is good to have some for future use as well. Cut two grey boards 10mm taller than your book and 10mm wider; being slightly bigger makes your book block easier to handle. With a hard bang, knock your book up so it is all straight and the spine is at a 90-degree angle with the rest of your book. It is a good way to make any sections that may have pulled back fall back into place.

34. When you have knocked up and you are happy, place your book carefully with the spine on the edge of the table, and place your weights/books on top so it is weighed down. You will now need to glue up your spine using PVA: put a thin layer of PVA glue all along the spine.

35. Leave it to dry. It needs to be completely dry so that it does not shift, so try to be patient and leave it overnight if you can, or at least eight hours. It will be touch dry in a few hours but it needs to dry completely.

Hello and welcome back! I hope you had a good little break, and you have left your book for long enough as well. Do not rush this as you will just regret it later, so if in doubt, leave it for half an hour more!

36. Now on to endpapers: these need to be in the correct grain direction and a minimum of 100gsm. If the paper is too thin it will just tear and cause you heartache and misery. Most high-quality printed papers and handmade papers are fine, just keep away from shiny wrapping paper or really thin papers.

37. The pattern on your chosen paper will determine whether you can use it or not. Most of the time the pattern goes with the grain direction, but sometimes it does not. At this point keep away from these papers – the pattern MUST go in the correct grain. You want it to be going head to tail, so if you have a patterned paper with a very obvious orientation then be aware of this.

38. For now your endpapers need to be 20mm taller than your book and 10mm wider (when folded) than your book block – so 10mm on all three edges. This makes it a lot easier to stick on and then trim after, rather than cutting it exactly and trying to line up. You may also find doing it that way your book is not perfectly straight.

39. Making sure they are both the same way if you have an obvious pattern, you now need to tip them on to your book – this means glueing them on with a thin line of PVA. Get a long piece of scrap

62 • BOOKBINDING AND HOW TO BRING OLD BOOKS BACK TO LIFE

paper and place it approximately 4mm from your spine edge and glue the gap. Place your folded endpaper on top and rub down, then repeat from the other side, making sure the patterns are both the same way up. Set aside under weights for thirty minutes to allow the glue to dry.

40. Now to cut around your endpapers. For this you will need your scalpel, ruler and cutting mat. Place your ruler between the endpapers and your book block, and make sure it is at the edge of your book block.

41. Next cut along your ruler and along the edge of the book. Repeat for all six sides. And Voila! Your book block has endpapers. It is getting there isn't it? You can see a book forming in front of you.

Intermediate Bookbinding • 63

HEADBANDS AND RIBBON

Take a look at a hardback book you have. Can you see at the head and tail there is a small piece of material? These are the headbands and typically these are now machine sewn and manufactured then just stuck on to the book block. They add a good pop of colour and just finish the book off.

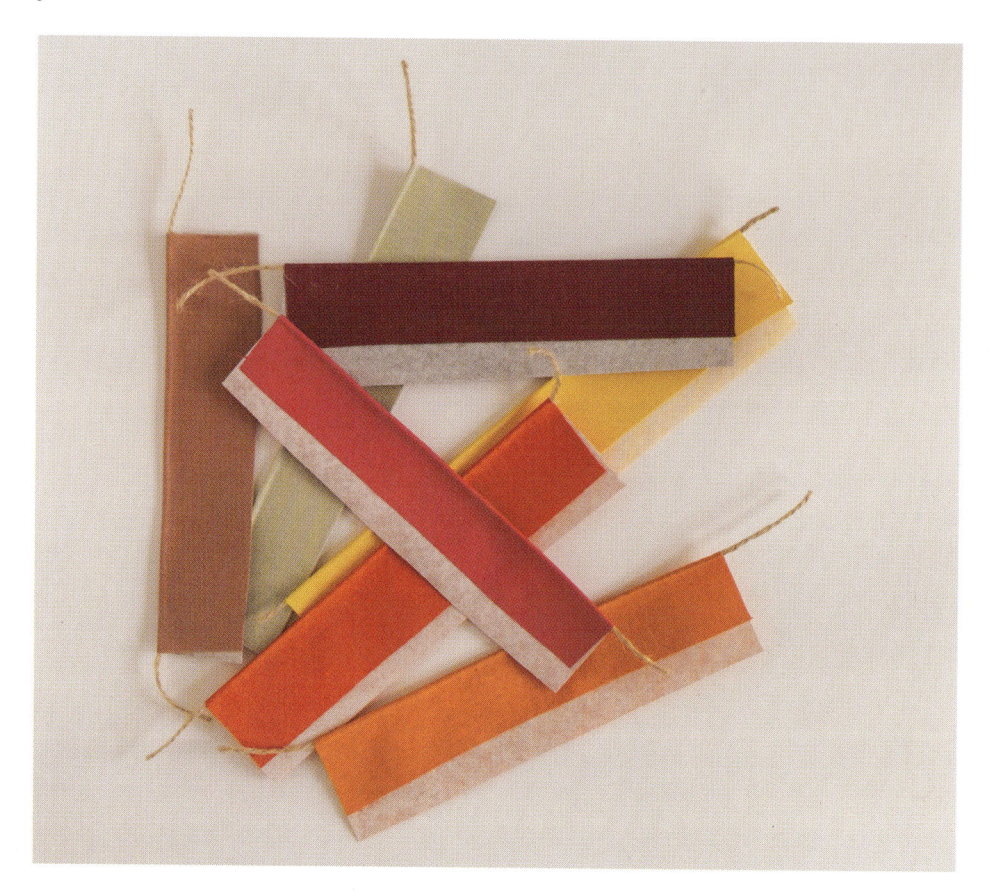

Making your own headbands is quite simple.

You will need:

Material – try to use bookbinding cloth so the PVA does not come through.

Thick cord – no wider than 1.5mm as you will be wrapping material around it and your headbands cannot be taller than the 3mm square you have around your book block.

PVA.

Bone folder.

Waste paper.

This requires some patience, so try and go into it calmly!

1. Cut a piece of cord roughly twice the width of your book, plus 30mm. You can make them as long as you want and use them on other books. I always have some made to hand and then just spend half an hour making more when I get low. It is an excellent use of waste material as well.

2. So now cut your chosen material the same length as the cord but 40mm high.

3. Glue up the material with PVA and wait about 20 seconds, this allows it to go a little bit tacky and more manageable.

4. Place your cord roughly in the middle of the material and fold over.

5. Now you need to use your bone folder to rub the material down and get rid of any air bubbles. The material needs to be covering the cord really tightly.

6. Use the flatter end of your bone folder to keep rubbing along the cord to make sure the material is completely stuck down and that there are no air bubbles left.

7. And there you have your headband; now allow it to dry. Whilst it dries you can add a ribbon to your book block if you want to.

8. Cut a piece of ribbon the length of your book diagonally plus 100mm.

9. Using PVA, stick 25mm on to the spine in the middle of your book at the head, rub down and allow it to dry for a minute or two.

10. Now to add your headbands.

11. Get your book and place the headband along the spine making sure one end is approximately 1mm in from the edge of your book.

12. Next mark up the end to be cut, cut the headbands with your scalpel or scissors and then cut another the same length.

Intermediate Bookbinding • 67

13. Glue up the spine with PVA and stick the headbands down. Make sure the cord is flush against the edge of the book.

14. Now you need to line the spine of your book. This is vital as it sticks all of the sections together. You will notice how much sturdier your block is after it has been glued up and lined. The kraft paper you will use to line your book needs to be 10mm shorter than your book block and then three times the width (approximately). You need flaps when you are sticking in your book, as this adds to the structural support of your book and also helps to secure your headbands and ribbon.

15. Glue over the headbands so the entire spine is covered. With your book on the edge of your desk, stick your kraft paper to the side and rub it down. You will see the sewing coming through and the lumps from the headbands and your ribbon – this is good, you want the paper to get in all the cracks and force the PVA into any 'holes' there may be.

At this point you have folded and sewn your book block, added and trimmed your endpapers, added headbands and ribbons and then finally lined up your book block. It is important you have done all of these things, as you need to be able to measure your book block and it be the final size.

Now on to the case: for this book we are making a flat back book, which means the case is made from three pieces of board rather than two as you did with the pamphlet binding. With this method of binding you are keeping the spine flat (hence flat back binding).

So on to your case, the measurements are similar to your pamphlet – keep the square in mind and make sure you measure twice and cut once.

1. You need to cut your grey boards so they are long grain, – so the grain is going from the head to tail. Their height is the height of your book block plus 6mm; the width is the width of your block MINUS

68 • BOOKBINDING AND HOW TO BRING OLD BOOKS BACK TO LIFE

3mm – this is because your case will have an 8mm gap at the spine so will push the board out.

2. Cut the grey boards using a scalpel and mat, then place them either side of your book block. Measure the width of the spine plus the two boards – this is the width of your third piece of grey board – your spine piece. This needs to be the same height as your grey boards for the covers.

3. So you now have three pieces of grey board: 2 x covers (boards) and 1 x spine.

You also need:
Covering material
Scissors
Ruler
Glue
Glue brush
Scrap paper
Bone folder.

4. Place your boards on your material, so the material is face down with the inside face up. Both of your grey boards are approximately 25mm away from the edge and your spine has an 8mm gap between

it and both boards. Placing your ruler along the bottom edge means they are all in a straight line.

5. Now draw around one of the boards, do not do both as we will measure as we stick, it is just useful to see what you are aiming for before any glue is involved.

6. Glue up one board – remember how you did it before, large circles going from the middle out – and place it in the rectangle you drew. Replace your ruler so you can measure the gap between the board and spine.

7. Now glue up your spine, place this along the ruler as well, 8mm from the board you just stuck down. Turn your material over and rub the board and spine down with the heel of your hand. Turn over and replace your ruler.

8. Glue up the final board and place it 8mm away from the spine along your ruler.

9. Rub down the last board and make sure it is all stuck down.

10. Cut the corners as before – you need to allow at least 4mm (if you are using 2mm board) and cut at 45-degree angles from the side of the boards.

11. Turning in the edges is the same as the single section book you did before, you just have the extra spine piece to rub down as well.

12. Glue up the material at the head or tail, then, using your bone folder make sure the material sticks to the edge of your board.

13. Now stick down the material between the gap by the side of the spine.

14. This is important so it is a tighter cover, it will not stick down

completely as the material is not stretchy but get it down as best you can then stick all of the rest of the material down and remember to WIPE AND SWIPE.

15. Do the same for the other side so your head and tail are both stuck down.

16. Now remember to pinch in the corners of your fore-edges and stick down the same. Always WIPE AND SWIPE!

17. So you will end up with this:

You have made your case, well done.

On to sticking in your book block.

18. Place your book on your cover and make sure there is a 3mm gap at the head, tail and fore-edge.

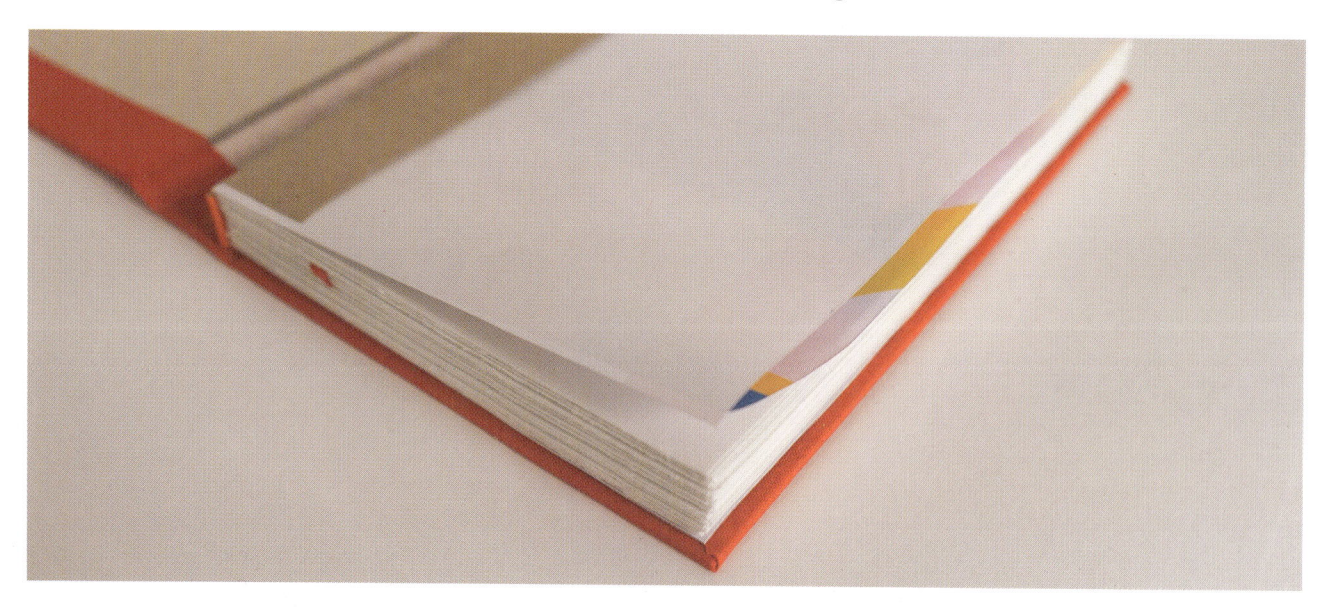

19. Now glue your endpapers – remember to glue in large circles from the middle out and glue under the flap.

20. Flap your cover over and push down, turn the book over and make sure it is in the correct place. You can 'slide' your book block at this point if you need it to move, just be gentle and careful.

21. Glue up the other side and do the same. Now your book is stuck in, take your bone folder and slide it along the gap by your spine and board for both sides to make a more defined crease.

22. DO NOT OPEN YOUR BOOK YET!!!!!

23. Place two sheets of paper in the middle of the endpapers, preferably blotting paper but just normal paper will be fine, you just need something to help with the moisture.

24. Place under weights and leave it for at least eight hours.

And you are done! Well done, be super proud of yourself with what you have just achieved. It is not an easy thing, but it will get easier with time and practise so try and do it again sooner rather than later.

Use the space below to write down what went well, what you liked and want to be aware of next time.

With this method of case binding there are a few ways you can cover your notebook, I recommend sticking to the full cloth for a few tries so you can get used to the methods. When you feel more comfortable you can start to explore the various ways you can cover your book:

Half binding
Quarter binding
Limp binding

HALF BINDING: this is where half the book is covered with leather (or commonly today, cloth), and it became popular when leather became too expensive. The leather/cloth protects the weakest parts of the cover at the spine and the corners, and then other materials or patterned papers are used to fill the gap. The half comes from a quarter of the boards being covered at the spine and then a quarter at the two corners.

QUARTER BINDING: here only quarter of the book is covered in leather (or cloth), so it is just the spine. This is even more cost effective as everything else is just left to be covered in other material or paper.

I carry out a lot of restoration work on these sorts of bindings; they became very popular and are probably considered to be the most recognisable 'traditional' method of binding books. I love the fact you can get a lot of colour on to the front of your book: you can go very traditional by using darker cloths and marble paper, but you can also make it more modern by using different sorts of material and then patterned papers.

HALF BINDING

1. Sew your book block as you have done for the full cloth binding adding your head/tail bands and ribbon if you want them. Once you have lined it and it is ready, cut the grey board for your covers and spine the same as well, so you'll have your three cut boards.

2. Take one of your boards and divide the width by four – so if your board is 200mm it will be 50mm in each quarter. In this case it means the spine covering will come on to the boards by 50mm, yours will be whatever your board measures out to.

3. Mark this measurement on each board on both sides, with a line so you know where to stick your material too.

4. For your corners you need to measure in at a 45-degree angle from the tip of the corner, the same measurement as your spine.

5. Make sure you do it this way and NOT by measuring 50mm from the edge of the boards out.

6. So both boards are now marked up for half binding (your quarter binding will be just the spine).

7. It is easier to cover your corners first with the half binding as you can handle your boards separately.

8. Corners: this is the same method you potentially used in Chapter One.

   a) Choose your materials, they can all be the same colour or you could have different colours on the corners and spine.

   b) To measure your material for the corners, make a straight line cut on your material, place your corners along this line so the line you have drawn goes along the cut.

   c) Now measure around your board 25mm and cut out four triangles.

   d) Glue up and work on each corner one at a time.

   e) Glue up the first corner and place it on your board, making sure it lines up with your drawn line. Now cut the corner as you have done with your other covering and turn in the same. Do the head/tail side first and then the fore-edge, remembering to pinch in the corners. Then rub down.

   f) REPEAT FOR ALL FOUR CORNERS.

9. Now you have your corners covered.

10. Next, the spine – this is the same for half and quarter binding so follow these instructions for both.

11. Get your material with the inside facing up. Make sure you have one straight long edge to start from.

12. Place your board along this cut straight edge and make sure your drawn line matches up all the way along. Measure out 8mm for your gap, place your spine, measure 8mm again and place your other board. Make sure they

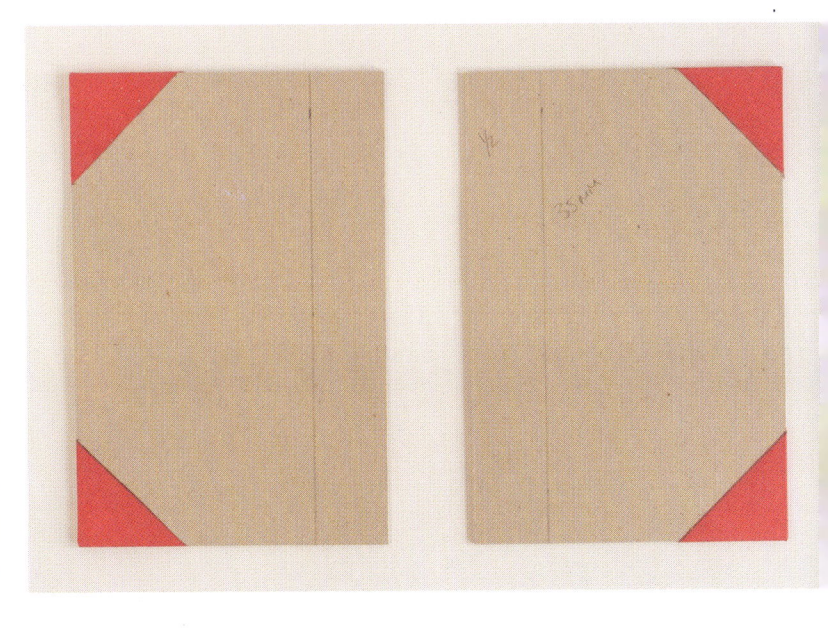

Intermediate Bookbinding • 77

are all in a straight line. Then mark up on your material the line of the second board . . .

. . . and also mark up your spine as you will need this for when you start glueing them on.

13. There needs to be 25mm of material at the head and tail as well. Once you have all of these marked out, cut out the rectangle of material.

14. Now to glue up your material and not your boards: this is a bit different because as a small piece, it is easier to do in one go. You will need to work quite quickly at this stage so please read ahead so you can familiarise yourself with the process as it is different to the

way you have covered any of your cases so far.

15. With your material on some scrap paper, glue it up using large circles as you do when you glue up the boards.

16. Remove the waste sheet and return your material to your working area. Place one of your boards on the edge of the material so the line on your board lines up with the edge of the material. Your line can be on the inside of your board so you can see it. Now place your ruler back along the bottom of your board and stick your spine piece down, 8mm away from the edge of your board, and then place your other board 8mm away from your spine – the line on this board should also meet up with the edge of the material. Rub the material down and then turn in your head and tail. Remember to rub down in the gap first to try and get as much of the material as you can down in the joint.

There you have your cloth covered half and quarter cases.

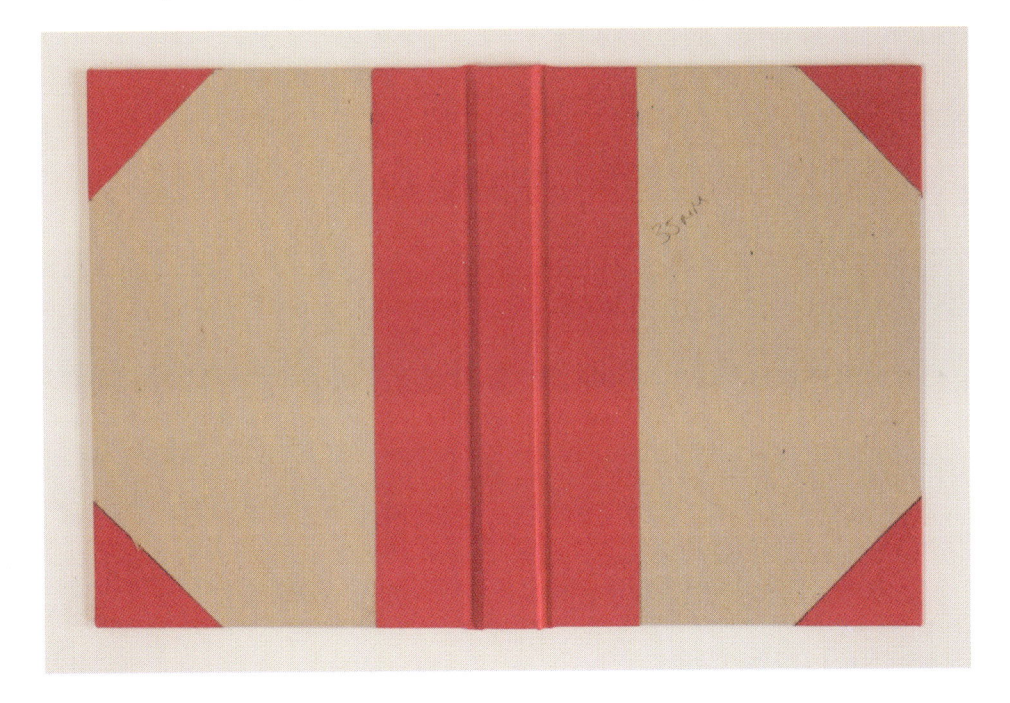

Now on to the filling: this can be done with either a different colour material or paper – if using paper it needs to be strong (100gsm minimum) and THE CORRECT GRAIN DIRECTION.

17. This is a different process for half binding and quarter binding, so make sure you follow the correct directions.

18. Half binding: you will need to end up with two pieces of paper or material like this at the end of this process:

19. If you are using patterned papers make sure you cut them out with the patterns going the correct way and the grain direction is long grain.

20. So to get to this shape:

a) Cut the paper/material into a rectangle that is 50mm taller than the boards and the same width – remember turn ins on the three sides.

b) Once you have this, lay the paper/material (with the grain direction going the correct way) on one side of your boards, make sure it is 2mm over the material on your spine, and then fold in the corners so the paper/material covers 2mm of the corner material as well. This is because you want the paper/material to go over the edge of the material, not butt up to it directly.

c) Cut the paper/material at the corners so you end up with the shape as seen in the photos above.

d) Mark this paper/material with a star and the side you measured it from with a star as well.

e) Do the same for the other side -MAKING SURE THE PATTERN GOES THE RIGHT WAY TOO!

21. Next glue them up and stick them on. Again, you need to be brave at this point and work quickly – so please read ahead until step 25 so you know what is coming and what to look out for.

22. To glue up the paper/material, make large circles and glue from the middle out. Your paper is going to curl up but just keep brushing the paper until it stops – this means that the PVA has been absorbed into the paper enough so it will stretch out properly.

23. Once all glued up, pick your paper/material up and place the long edge on the material 2mm where you measure up. Now lay the paper/material down and shift it until you are happy with where it is on the board. Once you are happy, rub it down with the heel of your hand gently as the paper may be weak because it has been glued out.

24. Then turn in the edges – it does not matter which order you do this in as there are not any corners to turn in.

25. Then repeat for the other side.

And there you have your finished half-bound cover.

26. Stick your book block in the same way as you did for the full binding.

QUARTER BINDING

1. So you have your spine covered as we did this together in the instructions for the half binding.

2. First cut two rectangles of paper/material 50mm taller than the boards and the same width as the boards.

3. Remember to make sure the grain direction and pattern are both going the correct way for each piece.

4. Glue up one side and keep brushing out until it stops curling

5. Pick up your paper with your fingertips – making sure you have the correct long edge along the spine material. Now place the paper 2mm over the edge of the material and lay it down so there is the 25mm allowance all the way around (roughly).

6. Now rub down with the heel of your hand – being gentle so you do not tear the paper.

7. Then turn over and cut your corners (as you have before with the corners of your material) leaving 4mm for covering.

8. And work the head and tail first, pinch in the corners and turn in the fore-edge.

9 There you have it, a quarter-bound cover.

10 Stick your book block in as with the full cloth binding and admire your work!

LIMP CASE FOR INTERMEDIATE-BOUND BOOK

This is an interesting method of covering your book: you need to make sure that you have sewn your book up and glued up the spine. Do not line it or add headbands as there is a different way of attaching your endpapers first.

For the cover you will need a thick card at least 300gsm, and you can cover this book in either book cloth or patterned paper.

1. With your glued up book block you need to add your endpapers; for this method we need them stuck to your book block not just tipped on:

   a) Fold your endpapers in half; they need to be 10mm bigger at the head, tail and fore-edge.

   b) Take your book block and glue up the entirety of the top page using large circles – making sure you do not get glue under the page.

   c) Take your folded endpaper and place it on the page with the fold at the spine and rub down.

   d) Do this to the other side as well, make sure your patterns (if you have them) are the same way up.

   e) Get two pieces of scrap paper and place them between the page you just glued up and the rest of the book block.

   f) Place this under your board and weight/books for four hours.

2. Once dry, trim your endpapers as you have before using your ruler and scalpel.

3. Do not add headbands or ribbon to this method of covering as it adds a lot of bulk to the spine. Line your spine using kraft paper as you have before and make sure it is dry.

On to the case:

1. This is a very different case to any others you have made as it is in one piece rather than three different boards.

2. Please read ahead and familiarise yourself with the process before you start.

3. Measure the height of your book block and add 6mm. Cut a long piece of card making sure the grain direction is going head to tail – this is important as you will be glueing material/paper directly to it.

4. Place your book block at one end of the card, leaving a 3mm gap from the edge of your book and the edge of your card.

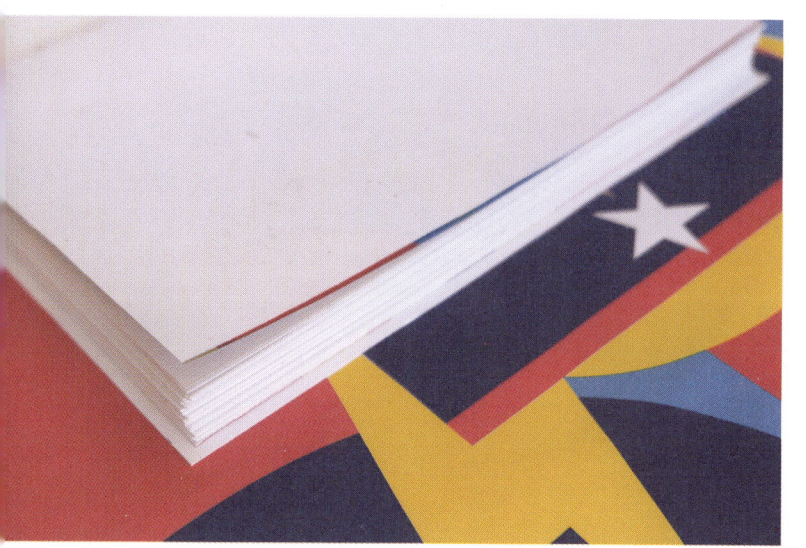

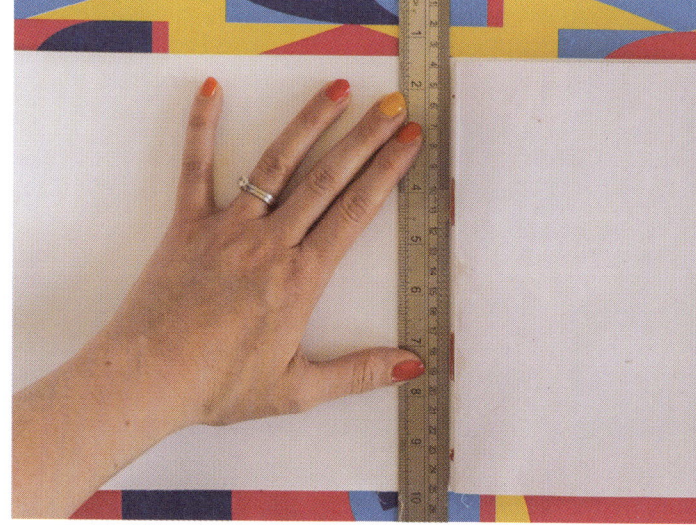

5. Get your bone folder and score along the spine edge on to the card. You will now have a line where you can fold the card.

6. Remove your book block and fold the card gently, making sure it is straight.

7. Measure the spine of your book block and add 4mm for turn in bulk.

8. Once you have this, measure from the crease you just made and fold the card so you crease the line.

9. Place your book block in the fold and place it down on your workbench with the uncut side down (so you can cut the excess).

10. Measure 3mm out from the edge of your book block and cut off the excess material. Make sure the case fits the book and you have an even square.

11. That is your case cut out.

On to covering: with this method, you need to be more careful when turning in the edges – as you are using card, not a thick board and the card can bend. It is really good to test yourself and your ability to feel your materials and how they are going to react. Try not to use too much PVA as the moisture will cause the card to get softer.

12. Glue up the card you have cut and make sure you glue up the outside of the card. Place it on your material and cut 25mm around the edge so you have enough to turn in as you have done before.

13. As with the 'regular' case you need to cut the excess material at the corners, now this is with a thin card rather than board so it is easier. DO NOT cut directly up to the card, you still need a little bit for the turn in, but you only need to leave about 1–2mm. Measure out from the tip of the corner 2mm and cut as you have done before.

14. Once you have done that you need to glue up either your head or tail and turn in. Remember, the card you are using is slightly more flexible than the boards, so when you turn over, make sure you turn over just material, not the card as well. But also make sure you do not fold the material back on itself. You need to feel with your fingertips and bone folder that you have gone up to the card, not over it.

15. Once you have done the head and tail, pinch in the tiny corners and glue up the fore-edges and there you have your case, all freshly made. At this point I would get on with sticking in your book block, as this allows the turn ins and the book to dry all together.

16. Sticking in your book is basically the same as the previous methods, you just have a slightly more flexible case so watch out for more movement.

17. Once you have glued up your endpapers and flapped over the covers, put waste sheets between your book and the endpapers to soak up the moisture.

18. Now as usual, place it under your board and weight/books and leave overnight – this one is a definite leave overnight if you can but try and leave it for at least eight hours. The longer the better really! It is also good to swap out the waste sheets halfway too.

And there you have your limp-bound case. This is a really good way to make lightweight, portable books.

So you have completed the intermediate bookbinding portion of this book and this method can be altered and adapted to different sizes. Have fun with your materials on the outside coverings as well as the paper on the inside. See what works well and what doesn't – it all comes from trial and error, don't feel too hemmed in by what is 'proper', just have fun and enjoy the process as it's a very relaxing and rewarding craft.

CHAPTER THREE

Upcycling Old Books

WITH THIS CHAPTER I will demonstrate how you can improve and personalise pretty much any book. These make great presents for friends, family and yourself.

Upcycling is a great thing, it allows you to breathe new life into old, well-loved books or just add a special touch to a standard paperback.

Give the gift of a book, just make it unique.

You will need:
- Scissors
- Scalpel
- Cutting mat
- Glue (PVA)
- Brush for glue
- Waste paper
- Bone folder
- Grey Board as follows:
  - a) Two x 6mm taller than your book and then 2mm thinner than the width
  - b) One the same height as the boards you have just cut and then the width of your book plus the two boards, minus 1mm
- Cloth for covering (this changes depending on how you are covering your book but we are just doing a full cloth case for now)
- Patterned endpapers
- Plain paper for endpapers
- Board for pressing
- Weights/books

With this way of binding books you will be adding your endpapers rather than sewing them on as with the pamphlet binding, and as such you need to make sure they are strong enough to take the pressure. With your intermediate binding you also tipped on the endpapers, but as you were adding them to a section sewn book the book block was a lot stronger and took some of the stress of the endpapers at the joint. With this method you will more than likely be adding endpapers to a paperback book that has been perfect bound, so the stress of the joint needs to be taken up by the endpapers and the paste downs, so we 'back' them. This means you are going to stick your chosen endpapers on to a thin paper so they have a bit more rigidity to them – this is an especially important step if you are using handmade papers. I recommend you do not go above 90gsm for the backing paper as you do not want to make the endpapers too bulky.

At this stage I recommend you read on so that you can understand what is going to happen.

TO MAKE YOUR BACKED ENDPAPERS

Fold both of your chosen endpapers and the backing paper in half, they need to be 10mm taller than your book block and 10mm wider (once they have been folded). This is just to make it easier to stick them on later rather than trying to make them fit exactly now. The idea is you are going to be sticking them together like this:

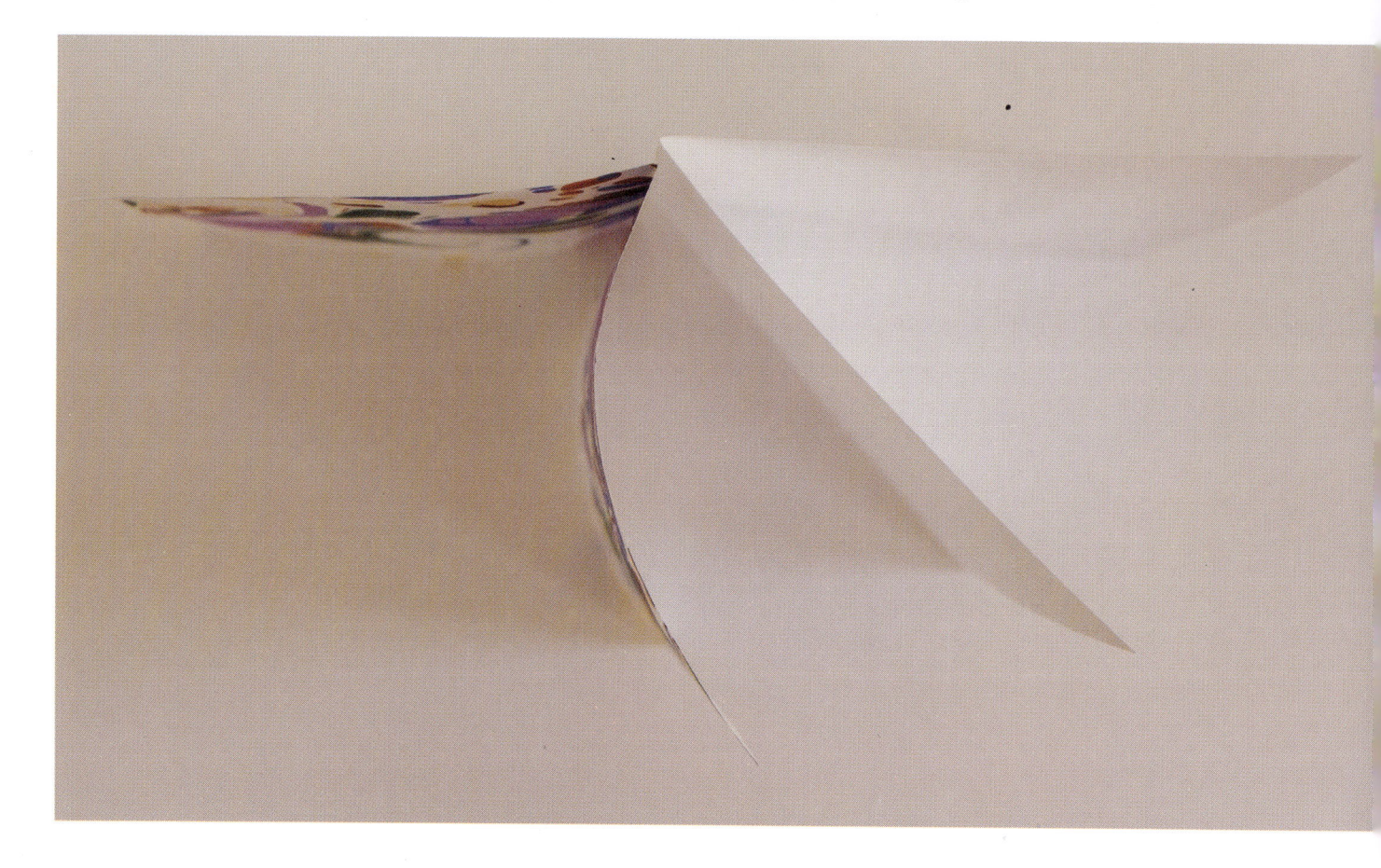

When you glue up paper you are adding moisture and the paper will start to expand (only a little bit). If you try to adhere something that is expanding to something that is not, it will force the paper that has not expanded to go crinkly when the paper that has expanded dries out. This is why we need to add moisture in the form of PVA to the endpapers and moisture in the form of water to the backing papers. By adding moisture to both papers you are allowing them both to expand and then shrink again when they dry out, thus eliminating the possibility of crinkles.

You do not need to soak the backing paper, it only needs to be a light covering of water that makes the paper start to curl in on itself.

1. With a damp (not soaking wet) piece of cotton wool dampen one side of your plain paper.

2. Keep rubbing in large circles until the paper stops curling (this shows the water has permeated all the way through the paper).

3. Now glue up the patterned paper – make sure the PVA is even and you do not have too much on there. Now wait for around twenty seconds or until the paper stops curling, as this means the PVA has been absorbed into the paper.

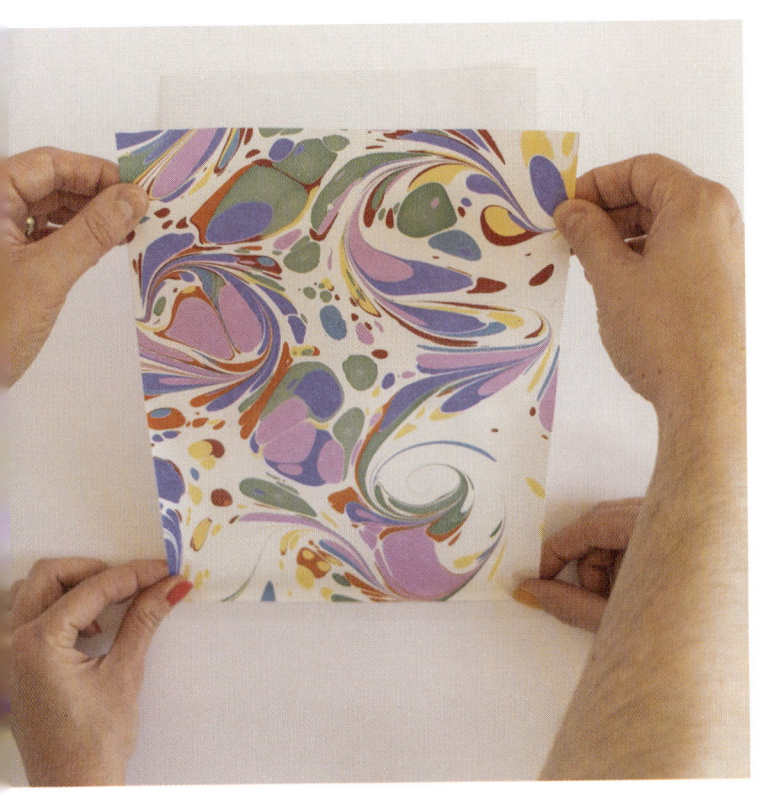

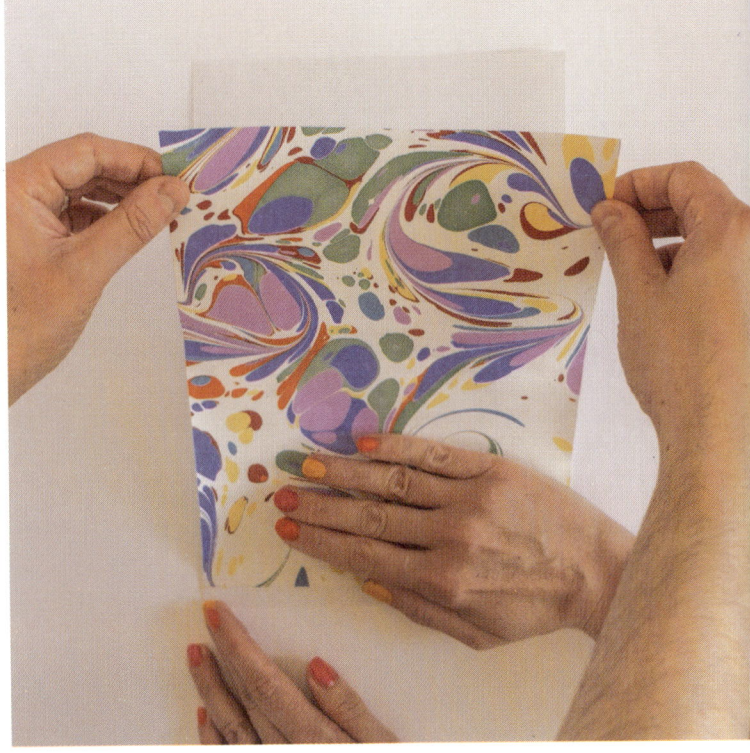

4. You may want to get an extra pair of hands at this stage to help you, especially if your book is larger than A5, as it can get very awkward.

5. Remember the papers need to be stuck together with the folds on the same side. So line up the corners of each fold and stick down, rubbing with the palm of your hand as you go. Rub down a little bit at a time, keeping the rest of the paper up and away from the patterned paper.

6. You will need to place this under a board and some weights or a large volume of books, and leave it overnight to fully dry. Do the other side and add it to the pile.

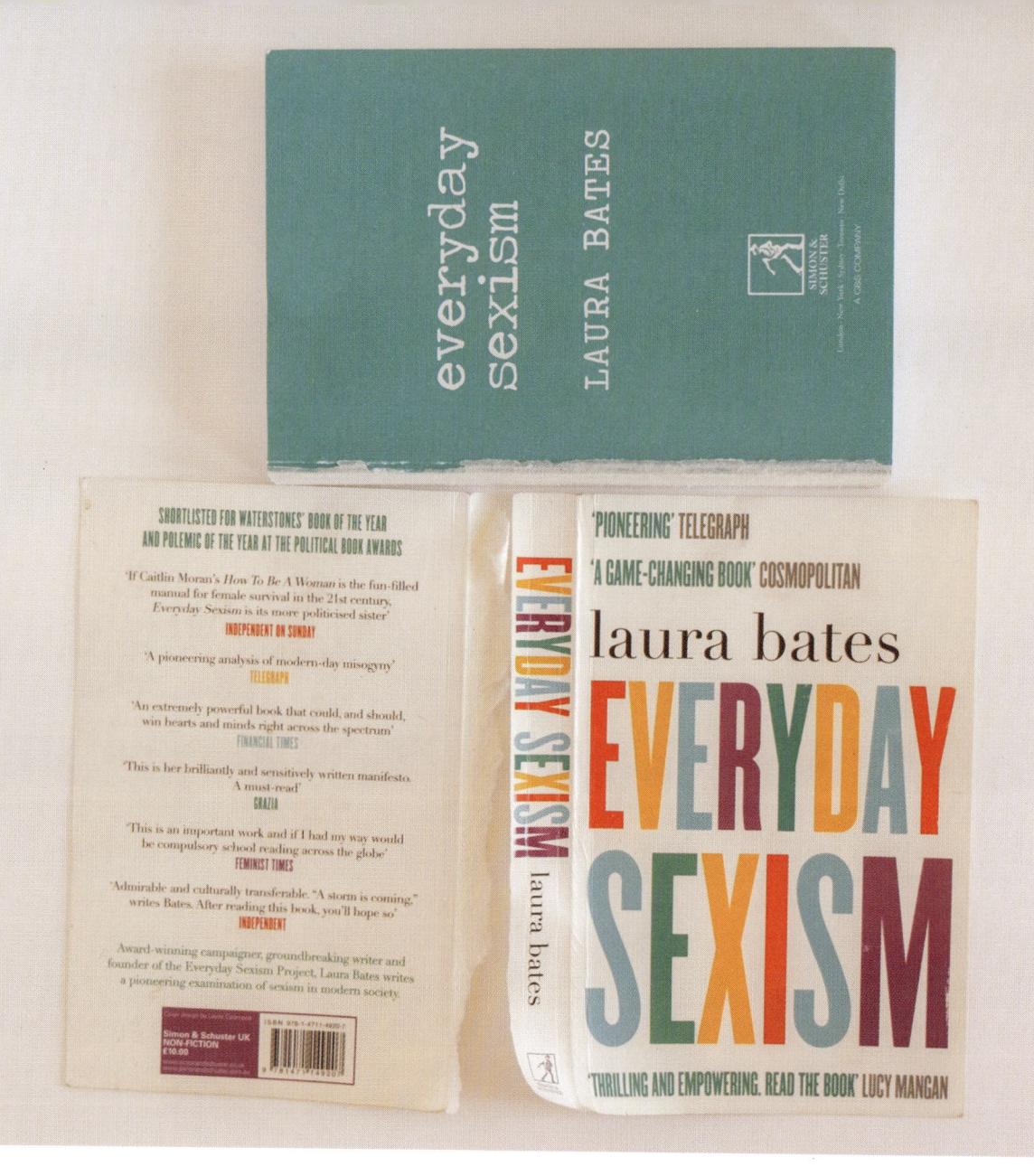

7. Choose the book you wish to upcycle and remove the covers. With a paperback just rip the covers off and peel off the spine as best you can (just the paper, leave the glue). If during this process you have removed some of the pages, just tip them in using a thin line of glue on the spine edge of the book and stick your loose pages down. It is best to stick to flat back books for this process so paperbacks are ideal.

8. If you have a hardcover book it may have rounded a little bit. To flatten this, place the book (once the covers have been removed) between two boards and give the spine a good thwack on your table. You are going to be able to get the curve of the spine out this way and force it back into a flat back.

Once your endpapers are dry, you can stick them on to the book block.

1. Fold the plain and patterned papers that are stuck together over so the patterns face one another (the spare plain page is just waste and will be removed later on).

2. Starting with the back, glue a 4mm strip along the spine edge of your book block and stick your endpapers down, making sure your pattern is the correct way.

3. Do this process for both ends and then place under your board and weights again.

4. After about thirty minutes they should be attached enough to work with. We now need to trim them so they are the same size as your book block.

5. Take this step slowly and change your scalpel blade as frequently as you need; it is better to use a sharp blade than even a slightly dull one.

6. Place your steel ruler between your book block and your endpapers.

7. Using the blunt side of your scalpel, make sure the ruler is along the edge of the book so you cut your endpapers exactly in-line.

8. Once you are happy you can cut along the length of your ruler – make sure you cut each side off completely, it is just easier.

9. Do step 8 for all six sides. And there you have your end-papered book block.

The next stage of adding headbands and a ribbon is optional. If you wish to do so please read on, if not skip ahead to the lining process.

HEADBANDS AND RIBBON

You have potentially already made some headbands in the intermediate stage of this book, if not here are the instructions again for you:

What you need:
- *Material* – try to use bookbinding cloth so the PVA does not come through.
- *Thick cord* – no wider than 1.5mm as you will be wrapping material around it and your headbands cannot be taller than the 3mm square you have around your book block.
- *PVA*
- *Bone folder*
- *Waste paper*

This requires some patience:

1. Cut a piece of cord roughly twice the width of your book, plus 30mm. You can make it as long as you want and use it in other books. I always have some cords made to hand and then just spend half an hour making more when I get low. It is an excellent use of waste material as well.

2. Now cut your material the same length as the cord and 40mm wide.

3. Glue up the material with PVA and wait about twenty seconds, this allows it to go a little bit tacky and become more manageable.

4. Place your cord roughly in the middle of the material and fold over.

5. Now you need to use your bone folder to rub the material down and get rid of any air bubbles. The material needs to be covering the cord really tightly.

6. Use the flatter end of your bone folder to keep rubbing along the cord to make sure the material is completely stuck down and that there are no air bubbles left.

And there you have your headband. Now allow it to dry out and while you are waiting you have the option of adding a ribbon.

7. Cut a piece of ribbon the length of your book diagonally plus 100mm.

8. Using PVA, stick 25mm on to the spine in the middle of your book, at the head. Rub down and allow it to dry for a minute or two.

Now to add your headbands

9. Get your book and place the headbands along the spine, making sure one end is approximately 1mm in from the edge of your book.

10. Now mark up the end to be cut, cut the headbands with your scalpel or scissors and then cut another the same length.

11. Glue up the spine with PVA and stick the headbands down, make sure the cord is flush against the edge of the book.

LINING THE SPINE

Hello again to those of you who have not added headbands or a ribbon.

Lining the spine of your book is important to the structure of the book – in the books you have sewn yourself it helps to shore up the sewing and also keep it all stuck together. In this case the pages are all fixed together with glue, so we need to line it to help keep the headbands and ribbon in place.

1. You will see there is a lot of glue along the spine of your book already – that is OK. What you do not want is flaky bits of paper from the old cover or any loose bits of old lining;, so remove these bits until all you have left is the original glue.

2. Now using brown paper you can make your lining. This needs to be 2mm shorter at the head and tail (so 4mm shorter in total than the height of your book) and then 40mm wider in total than your book's width. This is to create flaps.

3. Glue up the spine with an even coating of PVA.

4. Place the brown paper on your spine and try to make sure your book is in the middle of the paper so your flaps on either side are even and the head and tail have even gaps too.

5. Now rub down – if glue does come out at the head and tail be sure to wipe it away. Keep rubbing until it is all stuck down and there are no more air bubbles or blobs of glue left over.

The next stage is similar to what you did in the intermediate chapters of this book. If you have already done that, go back through your notes to remind yourself of any little pitfalls you may have fallen into.

We will be making a flat back case as you have done for the intermediate bookbinding chapter.

1. Cut two grey boards (they need to be long grain as well). Their height is the height of your book block plus 6mm, the width is the width of your block MINUS 3mm – this is because your case will

have an 8mm gap at the spine and will push the board out.

2. Cut the boards using a scalpel and mat, then place them either side of your book block and measure the width of the spine of your book block + the thickness of the two boards (so if you are using 2mm board it is the width of your spine i.e. 20mm + 2mm + 2mm = 24mm). This is your spine piece, it needs to be the same height as your boards for the covers.

So you now have three boards: 2 x covers and 1 x spine.

You also need:
- *Covering material*
- *Scissors*
- *Ruler*
- *PVA*
- *Brush*
- *Scrap paper*
- *Bone folder.*

3. Note the picture above: place your boards on your material as such, so the material is face down. Both boards are approximately 25mm away from the edge and your spine piece has an 8mm gap

between it and both boards. Place your ruler along the bottom edge to ensure your boards are all in one straight line.

4. Now draw around one of your boards, do not do both as we will measure as we stick – it is just useful to see what you are aiming for before any glue is involved.

5. Glue up one board – remember how you did it before with large circles going from the middle out – and place it in the rectangle you drew.

6. Now glue up your spine and place this along the ruler as well, 8mm from the board you just stuck down. Turn your material over and rub the board and spine down with the heel of your hand. Turn over and replace your ruler at the bottom of your boards.

7. Glue up the final board and place it 8mm away from the spine. It should all be in the middle of the material, with an even gap all the way around.

8. Rub down the last board and make sure everything is stuck down.

9. Cut the corners as before – you need to allow at least 4mm (if you are using 2mm board) and cut at 45-degee angles from the side of the boards.

10. Glue up the material at the head or tail and using your bone folder make sure the material sticks to the edge of your board.

11. Now stick down the material inbetween the gap by the side of the spine. This is important so it is a tighter cover – it will not stick down completely as the material is not stretchy, but get it down as best you can. Then stick all of the rest of the material down and remember to WIPE AND SWIPE.

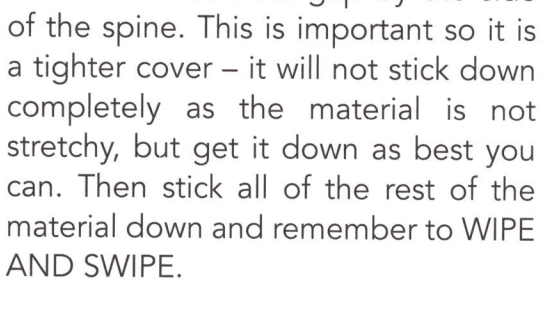

12. Do the same for the other side so your head and tail are both stuck down.

13. Now remember to pinch in the corners of your fore-edges and turn them in.

14. So you will end up with this. (See left)

You have made a case, well done. This is the point where if you have access to a finishing press you can do blocking (see stockists for where this can be done).

So now we need to stick your book in and you will be done.

1. With your endpapers you still have the waste piece of plain backing paper, this needs to come off. The easiest way to do this is to place your ruler so it is parallel to the spine and sitting on your book.

2. Next carefully make sure you only pick up the waste sheet and tear it off.

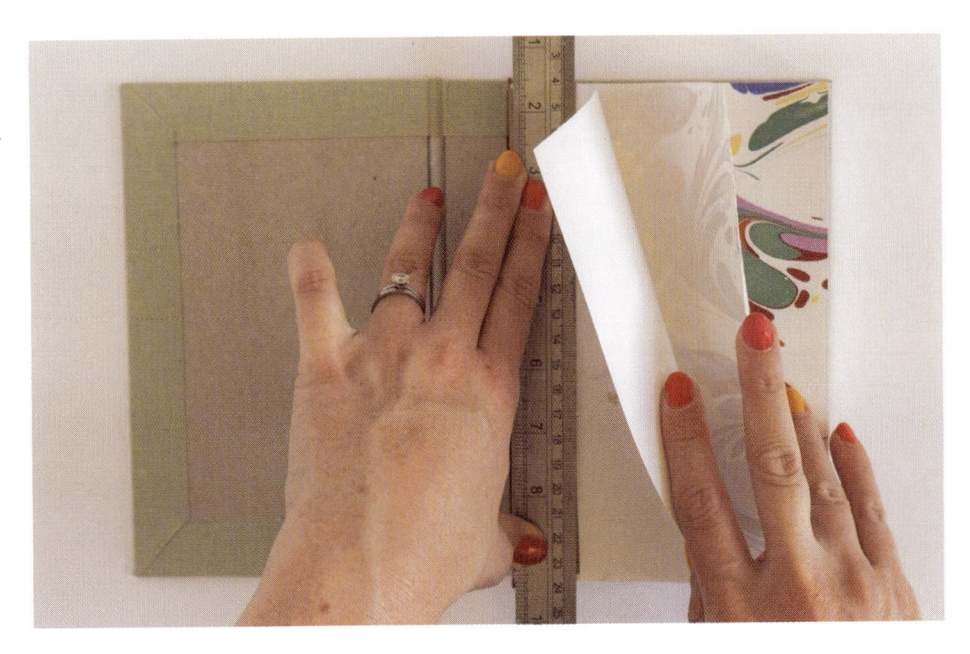

Upcycling Old Books • **99**

3. Do this for both sides.

   So now your block is all prepared.

4. Make sure your case and book are the correct way up (if you have had lettering done to your case make sure it is with the front of your book block).

5. Make sure you are happy with the position of your book: check the square is the same all the way around, feel if your book moves

when you go to flap over the case and remember to allow for this adjustment.

6. Get PVA on your brush and use those big circular movements you have used before to glue up your endpapers. Remember to go out from the centre, do not bring your brush back in, and get under the flaps as well so they are stuck down.

7. Flap your cover over on to the glued up endpaper, making sure the corners line up with the other board on the table.

8. Apply some pressure by leaning on the book, now turn your book over and repeat steps 4–8.

9. When you are done DO NOT PEEK! Please put the book under your board and weights/books and leave for as long as you can, ideally overnight so around eight hours.

When it is dry and you are happy, take it out from the board and weights. Now admire your wonderful handiwork!

Upcycling your old books in this way allows you to personalise a present for someone and also makes a unique gift. You also have the option to cover these books in the half or quarter binding as explained in the intermediate level, it is the same process – just be aware of different measurements.

As you probably do not have access to a studio to do blocking, another way to get the details of the book on the cover is to add a label. Normally labels are also blocked but you can make handwritten ones. These are also a very traditional way of labelling books.

They are best added once the book has been stuck in and has been left to dry. You have three options for labels: a spine label, a front label, or both.

FOR THE SPINE LABEL

1. Measure the width of your spine and deduct 4mm. You do not want the label to get too close to the edges of your spine as they may not stick properly and over time will begin to peel off, so just make sure they sit a few mm inside the edge.

2. The length of the label really depends on your title and the name of the author – some are very long and you may need to reduce them.

3. Once you are happy with your label, cut it out and stick on with PVA. Now this is important: you do not need a lot of PVA. You do not want the glue to ooze out of the sides, so definitely, less is more, with the label. The most important thing is you stick the edges down completely.

FRONT BOARD LABEL

1. The placement of this label is up to you. Normally it is placed in the visual centre – so not right in the middle but just a fraction higher. If you place your label on your book you will see it looks odd in the centre, so just move it up slightly and you will be able to see when it looks right.

2. You can have whatever you like on this label and it can be as large as you like.

3. Just remember when sticking it down, to make sure it is straight and you do not put too much glue on.

There you have your labelling options, they are a great alternative to blocking and you and your recipient will know what is inside the book.

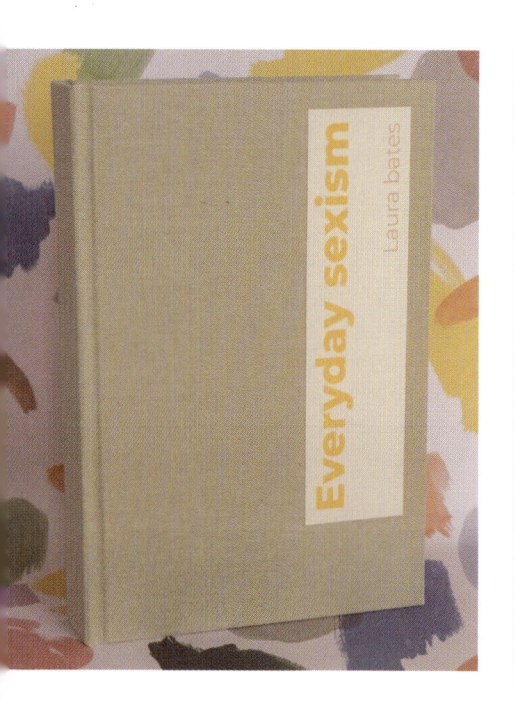

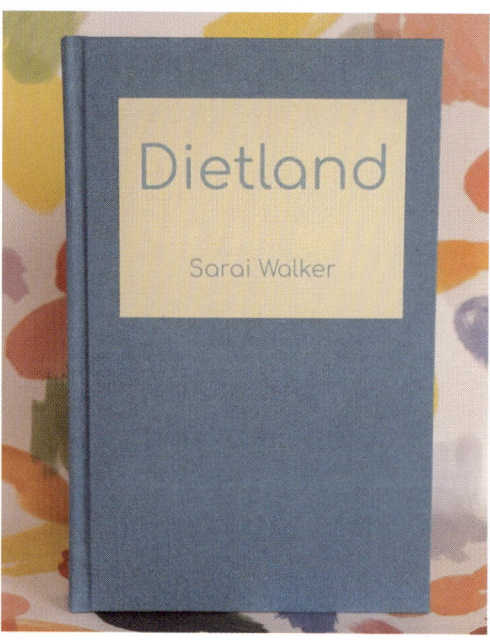

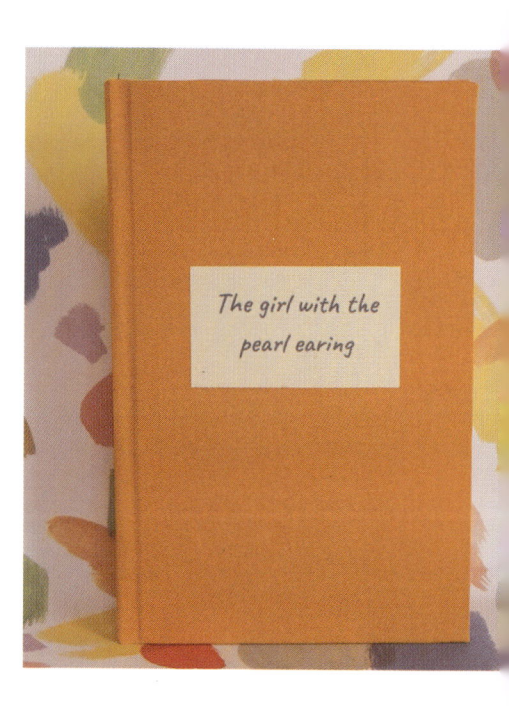

Use the space below to make any note for future reference for the next time you upcycle a book.

CHAPTER FOUR

Paper Repairs and Cleaning

CLEANING PAGES

One of the biggest things you can do to breathe new life into an old book is to give it a good clean. I do not mean to give your book a bath, as washing paper is not for the fainthearted and should definitely only be attempted by a trained professional. At home, you can use a smoke sponge to surface clean the pages in your books.

Smoke sponges are vulcanised natural rubber and were originally used for removing smoke damage from books that had been involved in a fire. They are great as they remove a lot of surface dirt and dust without taking anything else away from the page or leaving any residue behind. They are a useful piece of equipment and I have recently discovered that you can in fact clean them as well, meaning you can wash them and re-use them. Prior to this discovery I had always simply cut away the really dirty bits – ending up with a tiny bit of sponge after a while, so washing is amazing! But you do need to make sure the sponge is completely dry before you use it again – this is dry cleaning, not slightly damp cleaning.

Smoke sponges usually come in large lumps, so just cut off a small piece from one end. Smaller pieces are easy to manage and hold and therefore you reduce the risk of adding damage to your paper. I recommend you clean your pages before you do any paper repairs as well so the pages are clean and the archival tape does not have anything between it and the paper.

A great way to easily see the sponge in action is to mark some scrap paper with a pencil mark. Now using large circles gently wipe the sponge over the pencil mark, you do not need pressure or to do anything vigorously as you risk damaging already fragile paper.

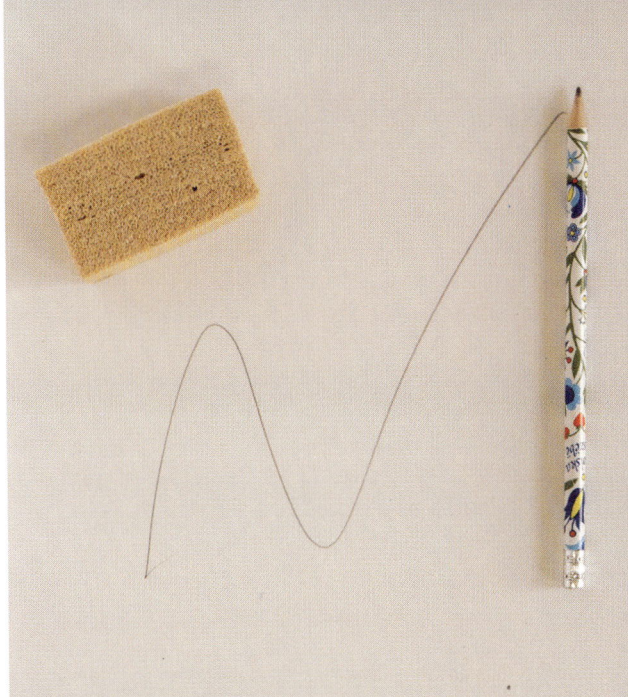

Your pencil mark should completely disappear! And your sponge will become dirty! The sponges are only able to remove surface dirt – so they will not be able to remove any ingrained dirt that has been there for a long time. They also cannot remove grease stains from handling. Although you cannot always see what the sponge is doing as easily as you did with the pencil mark, it is always good practice to give each page a little wipe over to remove any surface dirt that might be there. Doing this will help with the longevity of your book.

It is best to rub in circles rather than in lines because circles fade into the page more than lines will. Do not go beyond the edge of the page as you risk ripping or crinkling the page. Hold down the rest of your page so it is all under control. Doing it gently will also help to make sure you do not damage the page any more. An extra useful tool at this stage is a clean, dry brush. This is helpful to clean off any remaining little bits of dirt left on the pages or caught in the gutter of the pages.

PAPER REPAIRS

The most common problem you will come across when trying to renovate your books is the removal of sticky tape and then repairing the page again. I hate sticky tape, especially when it has been used to 'repair' a book. I have seen gaffer tape used to stick boards back on to books. Sticky tape is awful for books as it is full of acid, which is why it leaves behind a yellow stain. It can be difficult to remove but luckily most of the time it has dried out so much that you can just peel it off. There is not much you can do with the yellow stain, but by removing the old tape you can stop it getting any worse. The better way of repairing your page is to use archival repair tape – see my list of stockists for where you can buy this.

I will show you some simple ways to repair the variety of tears you may encounter and thus help with the preservation of your books.

This method is non-reversible; once the tape is down it does not come off easily, so make sure you are aware of this before you start.

Pages tear all the time, whether from overuse or just accidents. The easiest way to repair a page is using archival tape, which is acid free and therefore will not damage your paper. It will need to be rubbed down as well so you will need your bone folder handy. This tape is simple to use, but I recommend that you get used to it before you try and do a repair. I always tear the tape rather than cut it, this is because you want to try and keep away from hard straight edges. Slightly wobbly, torn edges fade into the paper more than straight hard lines do. The aim is to try and fool the eye into not seeing the repair fully. Take the backing off a bit and place it on a piece of paper, you will see how transparent it goes. If you use a long piece it does tend to roll in on itself, so make sure you work with small pieces.

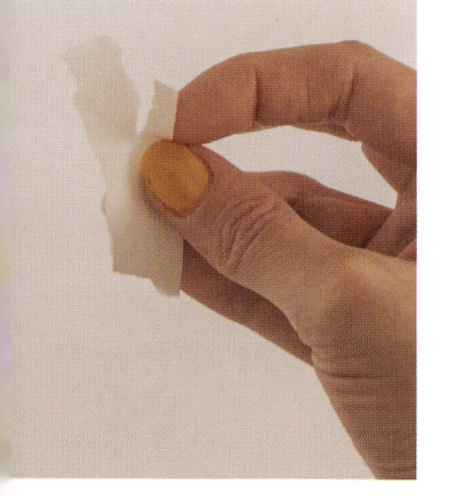

STRAIGHT LINE PAPER REPAIR

So you have a tear. Whether it is a full tear or just a little bit, if left alone it will just get worse, so it is best to try and repair it as soon as you see it.

1. Get your archival tape and measure it so it is about 5mm longer than the tear.

2. When you find a tear you will see that the fibres of the paper lie one way better than the other. Try not to force the page one way or the other, try it both ways and you will notice it lies better with the fibres lying one way. The surface fibres have been torn from the surface of the page on one side so those fibres need to sit back where they should be.

3. Once you are happy with how your tear is sitting, you can stick your repair tape down:

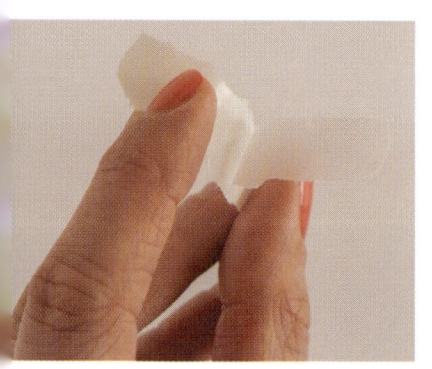

a) Remove a bit of the backing paper from the tape, enough so you can stick some down and be able to control it. Place the tape approximately 2mm before the tear begins, this is so you will definitely cover all of the tear.

b) To control the tape it is easiest to remove the backing paper as you are sticking the tape down. If you remove all the backing paper at once, the tape has a tendency to curl in on itself and can get rather tricky to control.

c) With a small part of the tape stuck down, begin removing the backing paper with one hand and rubbing the tape down with the other. Keep going until you have covered the tear, plus 2mm at this end. This is best if the tear is straight and one piece covers the whole thing.

d) Rub down with your bone folder and make sure you are gentle. You can rub in any little air bubbles or crinkles that may have appeared, but try and make sure these do not happen – do this when you are rubbing down with your fingers.

Paper Repairs and Cleaning • 107

CURVED LINE PAPER REPAIR

With curved tears you will definitely need to make sure the two sides of the tear are sitting on the correct side. It is sometimes more obvious with curved tears where the two sides would be sitting – be aware it is not always the same side all the way along. It is easiest to see this on a part of the pages with a lot of ink.

1. With curved tears you will probably need to use several small pieces of tape:

a) To begin with, tear off several smaller pieces of tape that will cover the whole of the curve plus 2mm at each end extra. Try not to have the pieces overlapping each other too much; you also do not want any gaps between the pieces of tape.

b) When you are happy with the size of your pieces, work from one end to the other and apply your tape in the same manner as the long single piece. Remove a small part of the back and place it where you want it on the tear, then rub down with your fingers whilst peeling back the tape. You may find in these cases that you can peel all of the backing paper off and stick it down in one go – be careful of this method though as it can be tricky and again make sure you do not make any creases or air bubbles.

I hope that these two methods cover you for most of your tear needs. It is the same principle if a whole piece of your page has come away, just use a small weight to keep the torn-off part in place.

It is different when a page has come loose and completely come out of the book, as you need to use the tape as a hinge rather than just bond two pieces back together. With a lot of newer bindings the glue will sometimes wear out and lose its adhesive qualities, so you may find quite a few pages have come loose in your favourite paperback.

Now a really easy way to reattach a page is to 'tip' it in. This means glueing up a page still attached to the book and sticking the loose sheet to it, so you anchor it to that page. This way of sticking pages in is fine, but be aware that the pages that have been glued together will not open as well as the others. So although it is a quick and viable method, there are better ways.

WHOLE PAGES RE-ATTACHED

A preferred way to attach pages back into your book is to use the archival tape as a hinge, as this allows the pages to have full movement. This can get a bit fiddly so read ahead to familiarise yourself with the process first.

You will need:

> *Archival tape*
> *Bone folder*
> *Scalpel*
> *Smoke sponge*
> *Cleaning brush*

1. You need to place your book so it stays open on the page you need to reattach. If it lies open where you need it just leave it open in your work area but if it does not you can tie it up. The easiest way to do this is to use cord, or something that will not tear the pages, to hold open the side with the fewest pages. This will ensure the book stays open where you need it to and you have both hands free to carry out the work.

2. Prepare the page that you need to reattach: remove any loose bits of paper from the spine edge and give it a clean with your smoke sponge. Using your brush, clean out the gutter of the book to remove any loose bits and all the dirt and dust.

3. Place your page with the spine edge off the edge of your bench – this is so you can attach the tape without it sticking to the desk. Use a piece of tape that is approximately 20mm longer than your page.

4. Fold the tape in on itself so you have a crease going the full length of the tape down the middle, this is just so you have a straight line to guide you when attached the tape to your page.

5. Peel off some of the backing paper and attach the tape to one end leaving a 10mm overhang. As it is going to be a hinge, half of the tape is going to be on the page and the other half will be on the book itself.

6. Peel off the backing paper and stick the tape all the way along the page.

7. Fold the tape in on itself so the non-sticky surfaces are touching. Now holding the tape down at either end with the 10mm overhangs, place your page on the book – remember to make sure it is in the correct pagination and therefore the right way up!

8. Make sure the corner of your page lines up with the book block below it and place your page down. Then keeping the tape folded, gently close the book – you need the tape to remain folded so the page will stick tightly into the gutter of the section. Open your book back up and give the tape a gentle rub down.

9. Trim off the excess bits of tape at the head and tail with your scissors.

10. You can put tape on the other side of your hinge as well to make it extra secure but this is not entirely necessary, especially if you have multiple pages loose in one area.

11. Then just keep adding in pages until they are all back in the book.

So there you have your newly hinged page(s). It is more involved than the tipping in process but does yield better, longer-lasting results.

ENDPAPER AND BOARD RE-ATTACHMENT

With the restoration work I do, the most common problem is that the boards are coming off the book: either coming loose or are off completely.

The main cause of this is that the leather or cloth has deteriorated so much it has broken. This is the peril of using biodegradable materials with books, although as most have lasted a few hundred years it is not that bad. They break specifically at the joint on the book as this is where most of the stress is located when you open and close books – their longevity depends on how well they have been handled. If they have been pushed flat or allowed to have the covers flap about, then more stress has been placed on the joints and therefore they are more likely to break.

This method is not necessarily a long-term solution or one for a book you use regularly, as it is more of a 'sticking plaster' than a permanent fix. But it is good to do in the short term to keep the book block safe and the boards where they should be.

This process for reattaching your boards is similar to reattaching pages that have come off completely as you are using the archival tape as a hinge.

1. To set your book up so you can do this process you need to try to make sure the board that has come off, or is coming loose, is level with the edge of the book – so it is at a 90-degree angle to the spine.

2. You can do this by stacking up some boards or getting a book which is the same depth, and placing it under your board. Make sure your board is butted up against the shoulder of your book. In most cases, the book block you are working on has been rounded and backed so it will have a shoulder.

3. Make sure your tape is a few centimetres longer than your book so you can handle it more easily.

4. Remember, do not peel away the backing paper in one go, remove it slowly as you rub it down with your finger.

5. What you are aiming to do is to make sure the middle of your tape goes in line with the break. At this point fold the tape in half so you have a crease line to follow, this makes it easier to sight it as you go.

6. Once you have gone all the way along your book, gently rub the tape onto your board. Be gentle as you risk breaking the tape if you rub too vigorously.

7. With this method you will need to use your scalpel to cut the tape at either end. So be careful, place your scalpel where you want to cut and pull the tape towards you rather than moving the scalpel – it is easier to move the tape so you do not cut the book.

There you have your board reattached. You will notice it does not feel totally secure but the repair will hold up if the book is sitting on a shelf and only being used once in a while. At least this way the book block inside is protected from getting dirty or moisture in the air getting to it.

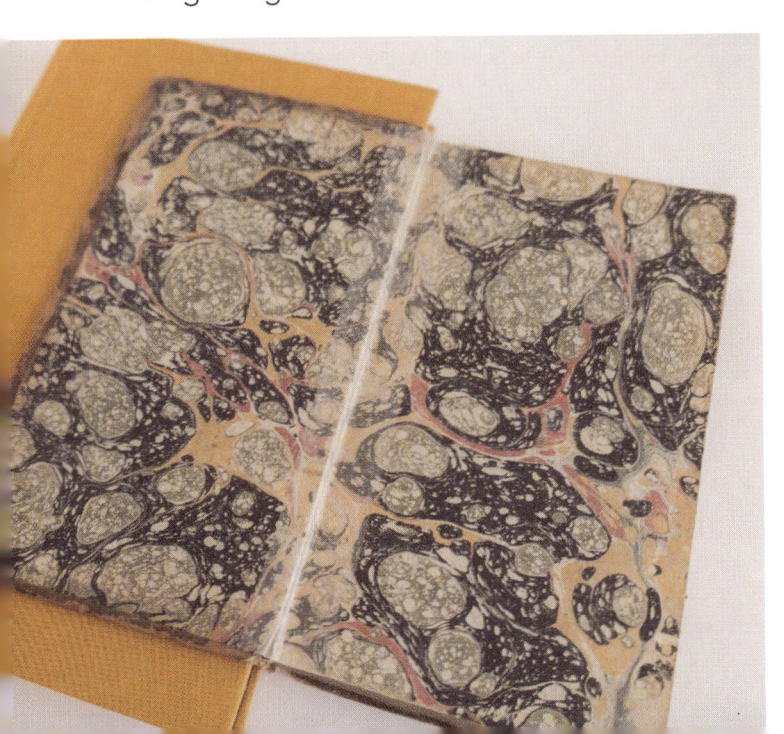

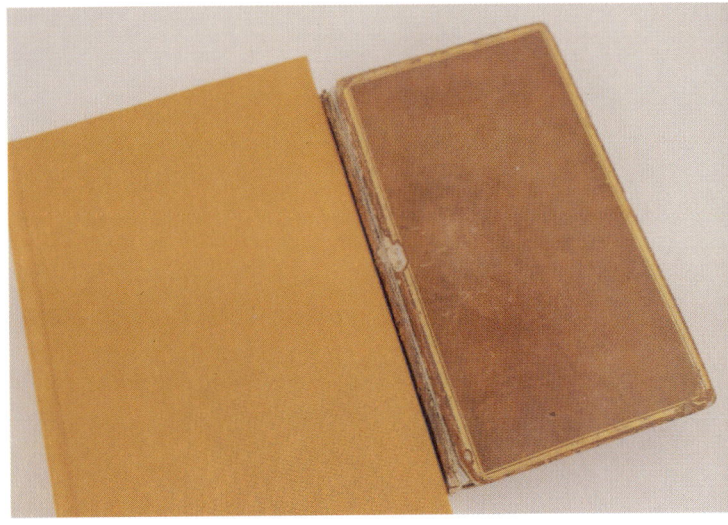

Paper Repairs and Cleaning • 115

CHAPTER FIVE

Weekend Projects

SEWING CARDS

This is a great project to do in a few hours on a rainy weekend. It is clean and simple to do, so can be done anywhere with minimal preparation or cleaning up afterwards.

Sewing up cards started as a way to save the cards we received on our engagement and then again when we got married. I really like it as it not only keeps all our cards together but makes them a lot easier to store as well. Another nice tip is to use ribbon from presents or flowers received from the occasion; not only a great way to recycle materials but it adds to the sentiment of the piece.

For this you will need:
Cards
Thread
Needle
Scissors
Ribbon
Safety pin
Pencil
Ruler

As with the intermediate book you need to have an even number of holes for your sewing template: two kettle stitches and two in the middle. With this method though, you will need to allow your kettle stitches to move in with the cards. This is because, as you will see, they vary in size so much it is inevitable. The main thing is to make sure the two holes in the middle go through the middle of all of your cards in the same place.

1. Gather all your cards together and put them in height order with the shortest at the top.

2. Now sort them so they all are centralised – you want the middle sewing area to be in the same place on all the cards – do not worry too much about the kettle stitches, but the two middle sewing points need to be in the middle of the cards.

3. Make marks on the cards with a pencil – you cannot make a template if your cards are not the same size, so you need to use the pencil marks to mark your holes.

4. Make all of the holes in your cards first, it will make sewing them a lot easier.

5. Starting from the bottom of your card pile – so the tallest card – place it on the edge of your table, with the outside fold facing you. Then starting from the outside of your card on the right-hand side, go in and out of your holes until you have gone along the whole length.

6. Pull the thread tight so you have about 20mm of thread coming out from the hole on the right where you started.

7. Now go up into card two through the kettle stitch and come out at the next hole. Next, to hook up with the card below, put your needle behind the exposed thread and pass it through so you are hooking your working thread with the stitch below it. Go back in and then out of the kettle stitch.

8. Now pull both threads tightly away from your sewing (so pull to the right) and double knot the threads, keeping them as tight as you can.

9. Go along the same as card two making sure to hook up the section below. Please note that you only pick up thread from the previous section, not all of the sections – make sure you go in on the left-hand side of the previous link.

10. Once you have sewn all along, pull your thread tight, then you need to link up with the kettle stitch below.

11. Place your needle between the previous two cards and pull it out behind the kettle stitch at the head/tail.

12. Pull through so you get a loop.

13. Now with the working end of your thread, go through the loop from the bottom up.

14. Pull the thread coming out of the card you have worked on tight, then pull your working thread end. All of the thread will come through the loop and pull tight, this makes sure that your thread does not become loose and your sections are really attached to each other. You are essentially tying a knot (if that makes it easier to work out what you are doing). Please refer to the intermediate bookbinding chapter for full detail and images to guide you if you need it.

15. Now keep going until you have finished all of the cards. When you get to the final kettle stitch, do a double knot as before.

16. Now to attach your ribbon: this is an aesthetic choice so you do not have to – I find it keeps them neater if you tie them up.

17. Place a safety pin or paperclip on one end of your ribbon – so you have something solid to thread behind your sewing.

18. Pass the ribbon behind all of your sewing and take your time, it can be quite tricky. Once your paperclip has come out from the sewing, you have threaded your ribbon.

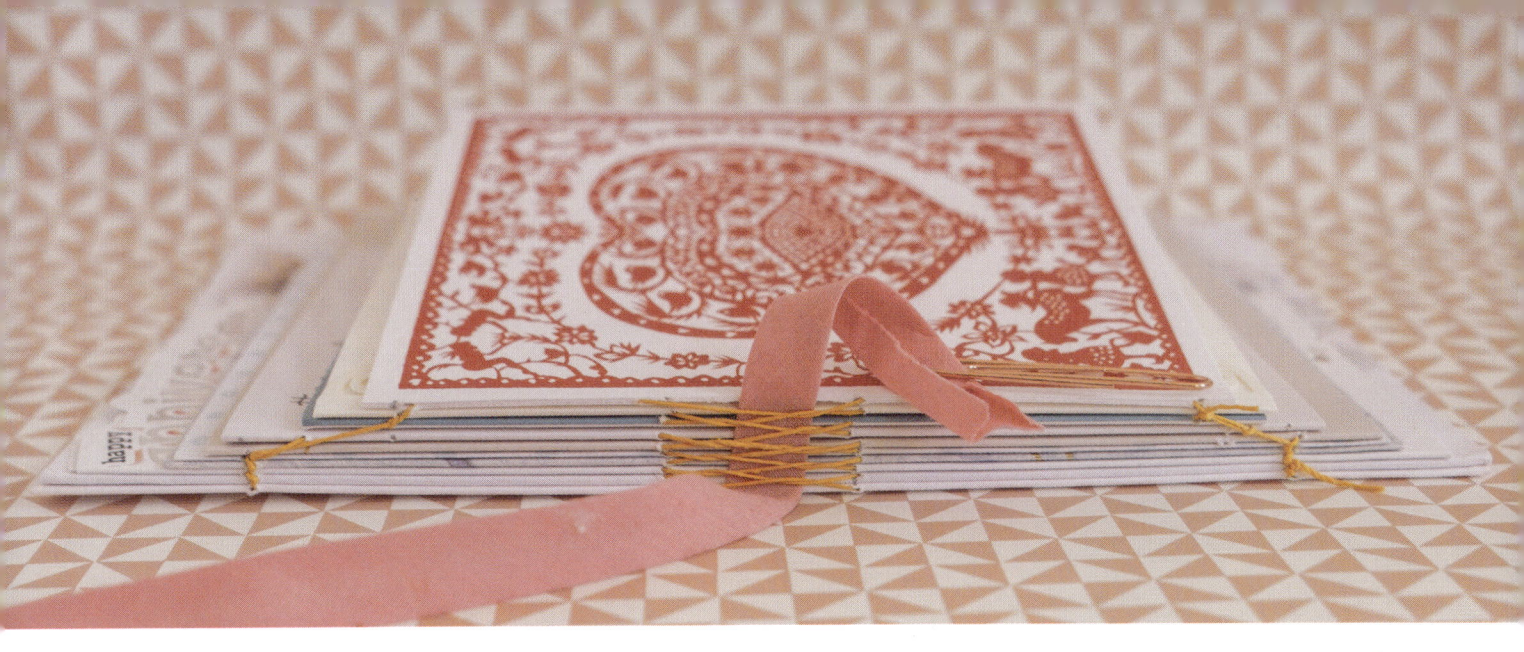

19. And now tie up as a present.

There you have your cards all sewn up – you can see how much easier it is to store them and what an extra special keepsake they now make. I love doing this to cards and have done it a number of times for friends and family too. Have fun with it as you don't have to have your cards in height order as I do, just make sure you keep those middle holes the same all the way up so you can have fun with the cards' order.

Weekend Projects

CHRISTMAS DECORATIONS

These are really fun to do yourself or with friends as a pre-Christmas activity. So, pop on the cheesy Christmas songs and let the mulled wine flow! They make amazing presents and show off your skills really well. They can be used as letters to Santa, writing down what has been received for Christmas, or as actual presents, with ideas for days out or fun activities.

They are really good for using up little bits of paper you have left over, so do not be set to the size I give, just remember to add the correct amount for your square depending on the size of your paper. They are similar to the pamphlet binding you completed first; they are just covered differently.

What you will need:

> Plain paper
> Endpapers
> Thick card
> Material/paper for covering
> Ribbon
> Glue
> Brush
> Needle and thread
> Bone folder
> Scissors
> Scalpel
> Cutting mat

1. Cut your endpapers and paper to the same size – I make my books approximately 10cm x 10cm, but as I said you can have them as large or small as you like, just make sure you change the final size of your case to fit your books.

2. Place your endpapers pattern side to pattern side, and place on top of your papers. Make sure you fold with the endpapers on the outside of the fold.

3. Shuffle your paper so it is all flat, as done previously, and fold your paper the correct way! Remember to fold it all at once rather than flat on the side of your table. You are looking for an even point.

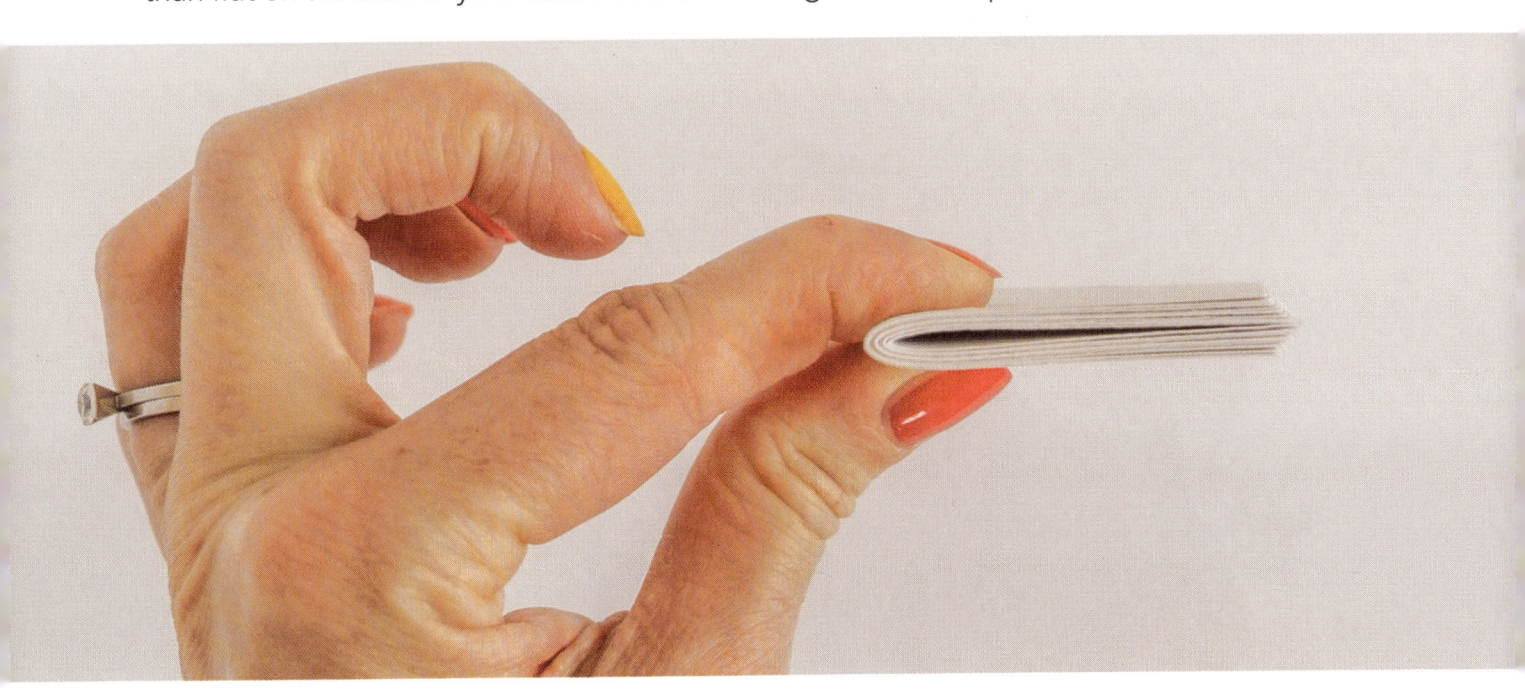

4. Once you have folded your papers you now need to sew them using the three-hole pamphlet sewing structure previously used. Remember to make the holes at 45-degree angles to your book block so the hole goes through the middle.

5. Once you have made the holes at even points, you can sew. Do you remember the sewing method? See if you can before you look ahead!

6. Going from the inside out to begin with, go through the middle hole. Then back in either the left or right hole, back out through the only hole not used yet and the back in the middle hole. Make sure your two threads coming out of your middle hole are either side of the thread that passes over the middle so the knot you make stays on the outside of the book. Do a double knot and there you have it.

Now for the case. This is a different method to the pamphlet binding you made. Instead of using tiny boards, I just make the case from a thick card as it does not need to be structurally that sound as it is just going on a tree.

7. Remember your square needs to be 3mm bigger at the head and tail and 4mm at the fore-edge – it is bigger here as the ribbon is being attached later.

8. Measure the height of your book and add 6mm.

9. Cut a strip of card going the right grain direction – for this it will need to end up short grain (so going from head to tail; as the paper will end up longer than it is tall, it is short grain).

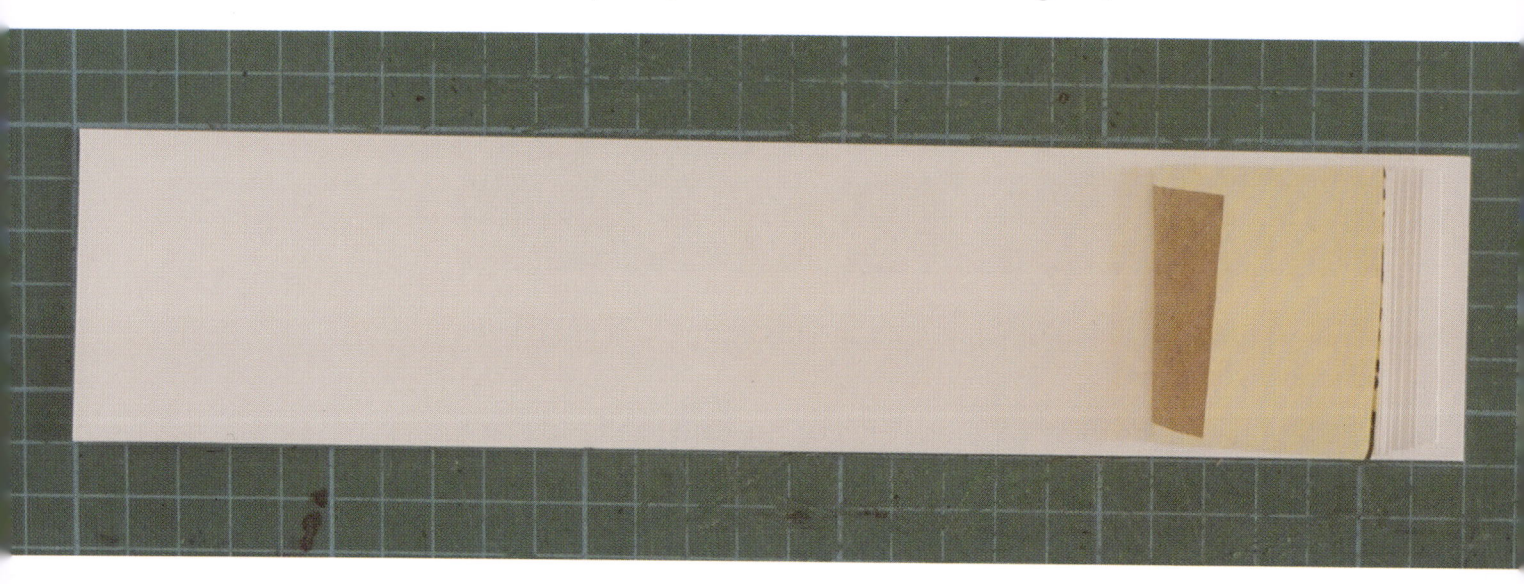

10. Once you have the strip, place your book block at one edge with the 3mm at the head and tail, and 4mm at the fore-edge – from the point of your book block.

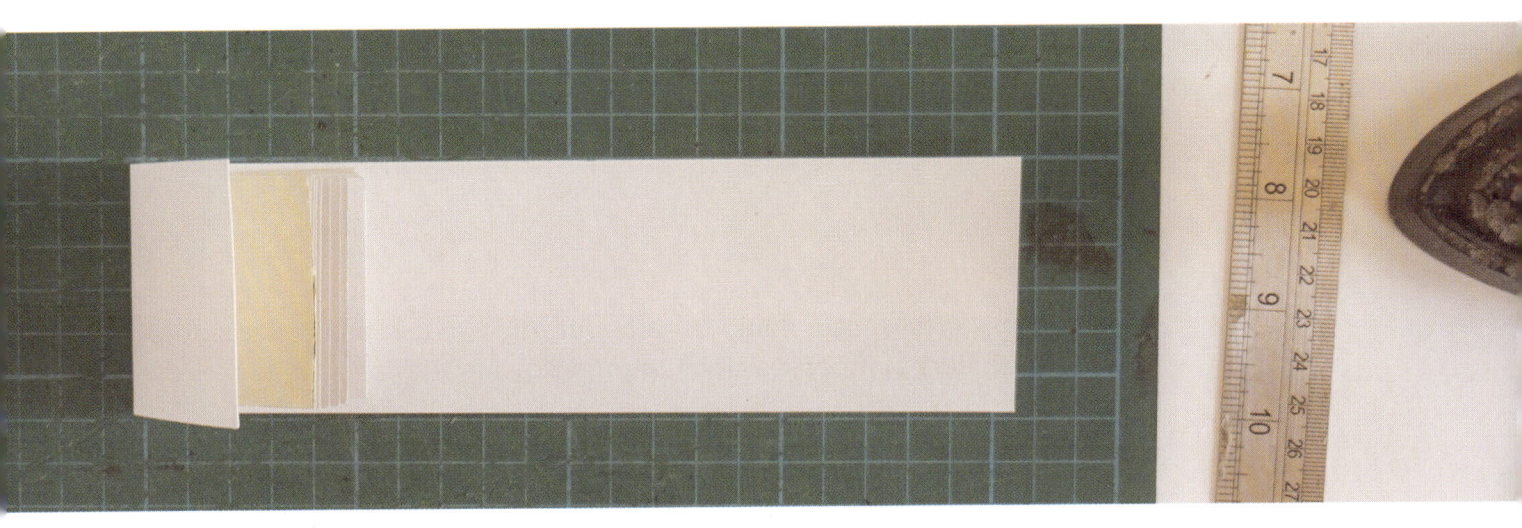

11. Now very carefully pick up the book block AND card, and roll it over so the book block is on the other side of the card. Making sure you still have the 4mm at the fore-edge, rub down so you make a crease.

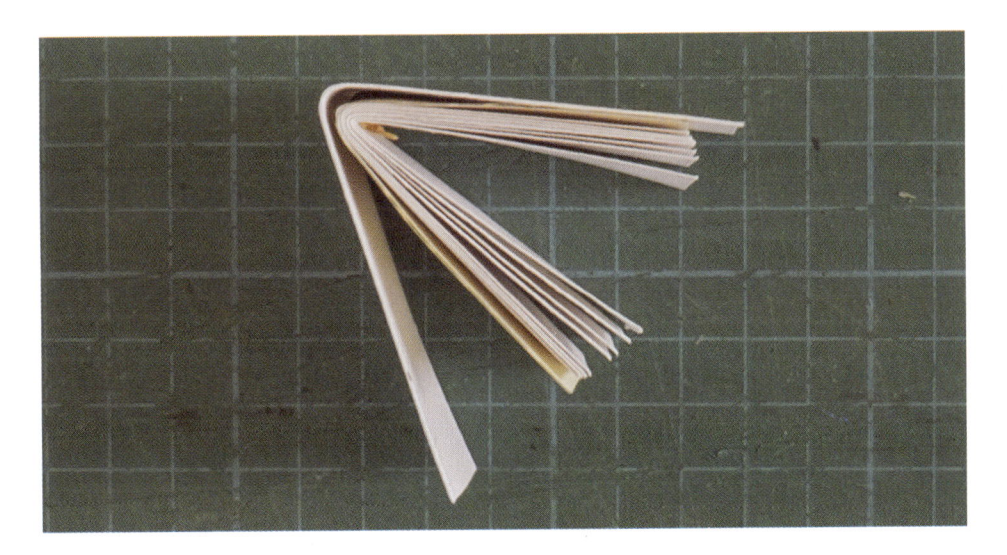

12. Next mark on the card 4mm from the fore-edge and cut. There you have your 'case'.

13. This now needs to be covered. Glue up the card itself and place it on your covering material – the turn in for a smaller book like this only needs to be 10–15mm.

14. Now cut your corners – as you are using card not board the cut can be a lot closer to the edge.

15. Turn in the head and tail first as usual and then the fore-edges. Please be aware that you must not be too rough with this method as the card may also turn in, so just be aware of how much you are turning over and also try to keep the straight line.

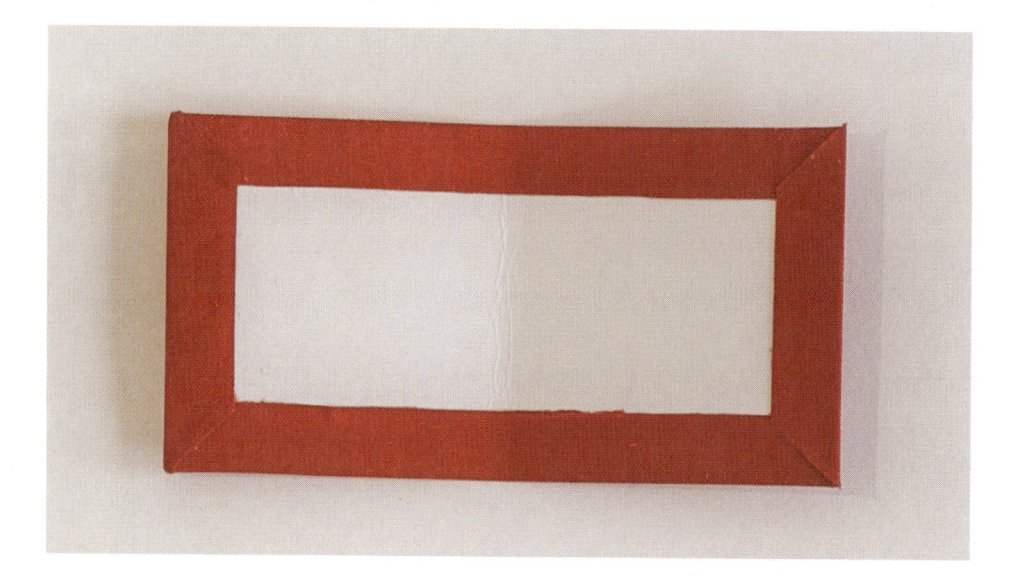

So you have a case for your book block!

16. Now to attach the ribbon if you want it to be a hanging decoration. If you are using ribbon with a specific face then make sure it is facing out. You will need to glue that side and stick it

to the inside of the case. I always leave around 40cm sticking out so it can go over chubby branches.

17. Place your book block in the case and re-crease the spine and stick in – this is easier than previous ones as you just need to glue up the endpapers and fold over the case.

18. Please place it under weights as you have used PVA. Allow to dry for a few hours!

And there you have your Christmas decorations.

Congratulations on your work, sit back and admire your handiwork and begin making more! They also make really good tags for presents as well, which the recipients can keep and use on their own trees the following year.